ROBOT

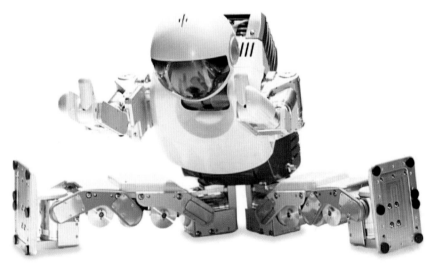

Wind-up
toy robot

Hobo bomb-disposal robot

PeopleBot
ready-made
robot

Evolution ER2
household robot

Lego Mindstorms
humanoid robot

Robug III
eight-legged robot

Koala ready-made robot

ROBOT

Written by
ROGER BRIDGMAN

Toy robot

Robotic hand

LONDON, NEW YORK,
MELBOURNE, MUNICH, AND DELHI

Senior editor Fran Jones
Senior art editor Joanne Connor
Managing editor Linda Esposito
Managing art editor Jane Thomas
Production controller
Rochelle Talary
Special photography Steve Teague
Picture researchers Julia Harris-Voss, Jo Walton
Picture librarians Sarah Mills, Karl Stange
DTP designer Siu Yin Ho
Jacket designers Simon Oon, Bob Warner

Consultant
Professor Huosheng Hu
Department of Computer Science, University of Essex

With special thanks to the Department of Cybernetics at Reading
University for allowing us to photograph the following robots:
4tl, 4tr, 6bl, 6–7bc, 14–15bc, 16clt, 16clb, 17tl, 17c, 17br, 17cr,
21bc, 29tl, 29br, 32–33bc, 33cl, 34bl, 56–57c, 59tr

Swarm robots

Flakey

Wakamaru

Asimo

This Eyewitness ® Guide has been conceived by
Dorling Kindersley Limited and Editions Gallimard

First American Edition, 2004

Published in the United States by
DK Publishing, Inc.
375 Hudson Street
New York, New York 10014

04 05 06 07 08 10 9 8 7 6 5 4 3 2 1

A Cataloging-in-Publication record for this book
is available from the Library of Congress.

ISBN 0-7566-0254-8

Color reproduction by Colourscan, Singapore
Printed in China by Toppan Printing Co., (Shenzhen) Ltd.

Discover more at
www.dk.com

Lego Artbot

Amigobots

Contents

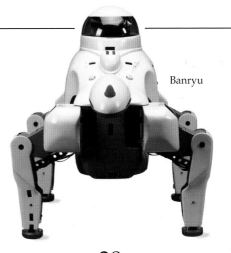

Banryu

What is a robot?

A TRUE ROBOT IS any machine that can move around and do different tasks without human help. It does not have to look like a human being. In fact, a machine that actually looks and behaves just like a real person is still a distant dream. Remote-controlled machines are not true robots because they need people to guide them. Automatic machines are not true robots because they can do only one specific job. Computers are not true robots because they cannot move. But these machines are still an important part of robotics. They all help to develop the basic abilities of true robots: movement, senses, and intelligence.

Robot character
from *Rossum's
Universal Robots*

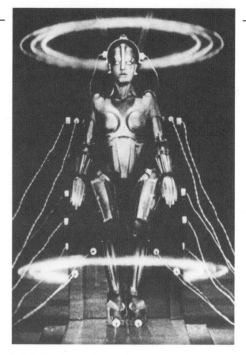

MECHANICAL MOVIE STARS
This mechanical woman was one of the first robots in film. She was created in the 1926 silent film *Metropolis* by German director Fritz Lang. Movies can make almost anything seem real, and fiction and fantasy have helped inspire the development of robots in the real world.

ENTER THE ROBOT
The word "robot" was coined by Czech playwright Karel Capek in his play *Rossum's Universal Robots*, about humanlike machines. Robot comes from the Czech word *robota*, which means hard work or forced labor. Capek wrote the play in 1920, but "robot" did not enter the English language until 1923, when the play was first staged in London.

Infrared
receivers

Infrared
emitters

BASIC BITS
The simplest mobile robots are made up of several basic units that provide them with movement, senses, and intelligence. This robot moves on electrically driven wheels and uses infrared light for sensing. Its intelligence comes from a tiny onboard computer housed on the main circuit board.

Screws for the
front wheel

Main circuit board

Front wheel

Main chassis

FINISHED PERFORMER
When assembled, the basic units form a simple but agile robot (left). It can move around by itself and avoid obstacles without human help. It was built to show off the art of robotics at Thinktank, the Birmingham Museum of Science and Discovery, UK.

Power supply unit

FACTORY WORKERS

Most of the world's million or so robots are not true robots, but fixed arms that help to make things in factories. The arms that weld car bodies led the way for industrial robotics. Cars made this way are cheaper and more reliable than those made by humans, because industrial robots can work more accurately and for longer.

With a body packed full of computers, motor drives, and batteries, P2 stood over 6 ft (1.8 m) tall and weighed in at a hefty 460 lb (210 kg).

SHEAR SKILL

Like most robots used in industry, the University of Western Australia's sheep-shearing robot is designed to be flexible. It can safely shear the wool off a live sheep. It needs power to work fast, as well as sensitivity to avoid hurting the sheep.

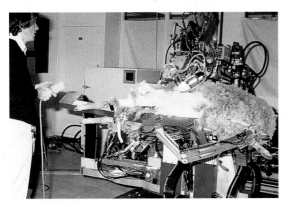

Infrared receivers

Back wheel

Nuts and bolts

Motor chassis

Cable to link circuit board with power supply

HUMANOID ROBOTS

P2, launched in 1996, was the first autonomous (independent) humanoid robot. Many people think that all robots should look like humans, but robots are usually just the best shape for the job they are built to do. Robots of the future, however, will need to work alongside people in houses and offices, so a humanoid body may be best.

Powerful, flexible legs enabled P2 to walk, push a cart, and climb stairs.

Battery pack

Back wheel

Fictional robots

C-3PO as he appeared in
The Empire Strikes Back,
Episode V of the
Star Wars saga, 1980

IN THE WORLD OF robotics, there is a close relationship between imagination and technology. Many people get their first ideas about robots from books, movies, and television. Authors and filmmakers have long been fascinated by the idea of machines that behave like people, and have woven fantasy worlds around them. Improbable as they are, these works of fiction have inspired scientists and engineers to try to imitate them. Their attempts have so far fallen short of the android marvels of science fiction. However, robots are getting more human, and may inspire even more adventurous fictional creations.

His golden outer shell was added by Anakin's mother Shmi. Before that, he had to put up with being naked, with all his parts and wires showing.

KEEPING THE PEACE
C-3PO, the world's best-known humanoid robot, first appeared in the 1977 film *Star Wars*. In the movie, he was built from scrap by a nine-year-old boy named Anakin Skywalker on the planet Tatooine. C-3PO was designed as a "protocol droid" to keep the peace between politicians from different planets. He understands the cultures and languages of many colonies.

The shell helped to protect his inner workings from sandstorms on the planet Tatooine.

Wind-up Robby the Robot toy, made in Japan

THE FUTUREMEN
Grag, the metal robot, is one of the crew in a series of book-length magazines called *Captain Future, Wizard of Science*. The series was created in 1940 by US author Edmond Hamilton, and it ran until 1951. Captain Future's crew, the Futuremen, also includes Otho, the synthetic humanoid robot, and Simon Wright, the living brain.

BOX ON LEGS
In the 1956 film *Forbidden Planet*, Captain Adams lands on a distant planet and is greeted by Robby the Robot. "Do you speak English?" Robby asks. "If not, I speak 187 other languages and their various dialects." Robby the Robot's box-on-legs look became the model for many early toy robots.

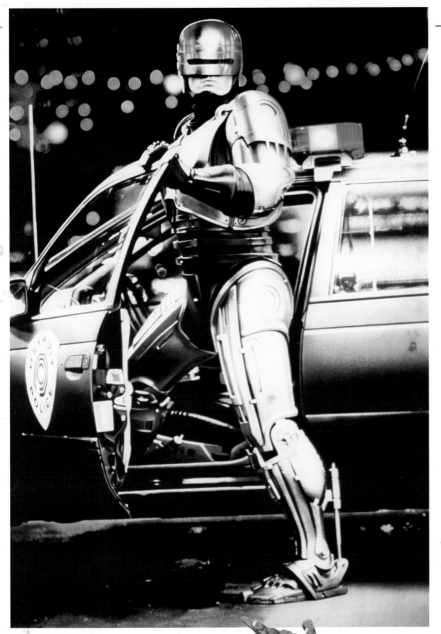

Robocop first appeared in 1987, in the futuristic film of the same name. Robocop is created when the brain of police officer Alex Murphy (killed by a gang) is combined with robot parts to produce the ultimate "cop." Robocop works with terrifying effectiveness 24 hours a day and can record everything that happens, providing unshakable evidence to convict criminals.

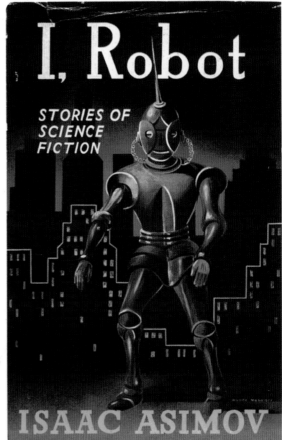

ROBOT RULES
US writer Isaac Asimov published a collection of short stories called *I, Robot* in 1950. Among the stories is one called *Liar!* It sets out three laws of robotics. The laws are intended to ensure that robots protect their owners, other humans, and also themselves—as far as possible.

ON A MISSION
The British television series *Doctor Who* (1963–1989) featured a race of mutant creatures called Daleks. Each was encased within a gliding, robotic "tank." With their metallic cries of "Exterminate, exterminate!" their mission was to conquer the galaxy and dominate all life, but their plans were always foiled by the Doctor. *Doctor Who* also featured a robotic dog called K-9 and ruthless androids called Cybermen, but it was the Daleks who made the greatest impression.

Johnny Five Alive, a robot on the run

STARSTRUCK
Robot Number 5, or Johnny Five Alive, is the star of the 1986 film *Short Circuit*. The comical robots for the film were created by Syd Mead. Johnny Five Alive is a military robot who gets struck by lightning, develops humanlike self-awareness, and escapes to avoid reprogramming.

9

Robot ancestors

Mechanical creatures, wind-up toys, and dolls that move have all played a part in the development of robotics. The earliest models were not true robots because they had no intelligence and could not be instructed to do different tasks. These machines are called automata, from the same Greek word that gives us "automatic." From the 16th century onward, automata were made following mechanical principles originally used by clockmakers to produce actions such as the striking of bells. These techniques were adapted, particularly in Japan and France, to produce moving figures that would astonish anyone who saw them.

VAUCANSON, né en 170_ créa les _/_ tomates en 1738, meurt en 1782.

FAKE FLUTIST
One of the 18th century's most famous automata was a flute-player created by French engineer Jacques de Vaucanson. Built in 1783, the automaton's wooden fingers and artificial lungs were moved by a clever mechanism to play 12 different tunes on a real flute. It worked so well that some people thought there must be a real player concealed inside.

EARLY BIRD
The first known automaton was an artificial pigeon built in about 400 BC by ancient Greek scientist Archytas of Tarentum. The pigeon was limited to "flying" around on an arm driven by steam or air. Archytas probably built his pigeon as a way of finding out more about the mathematics of machines.

Openings at the top of the organ pipes allow sound to escape.

The handle is turned to operate the pipe-and-bellows mechanism of the organ.

TIPPOO'S TIGER
This mechanical wooden tiger doubles as an elaborate case for a toy organ. It was built in about 1795 for the Indian ruler Tippoo Sultan, whose nickname was the Tiger of Mysore. When the handle on the tiger's shoulder is turned, the model comes to life. The tiger growls as it savages a British soldier, and the soldier feebly waves his arm and cries out. The sounds are produced by the organ inside the tiger.

Air pumped into the bellows is expelled as a shriek and a roar.

CHESS CHEAT

This 18th-century illustration shows a fake chess-playing machine known as the Turk. German inventor Wolfgang von Kempelen built the chess-playing automaton in 1769. It could play chess with a human and win! It seems certain, however, that the movements of the chess pieces were controlled by a human player.

An operator hidden inside may have played the Turk's moves.

The Turk, with its possible secret revealed

TEA MACHINE

Between 1615 and 1865, puppets called Karakuri were developed in Japan. They included dolls that served tea. The host would place a cup on a tray held by the doll. This triggered the doll to move forward. It would stop when a guest picked up the cup. When the cup was put back on the tray, the doll would turn around and trundle back to its starting place.

The doll is driven by clockwork with a spring made from part of a whale.

When the large cat turns the handle, the small cat kicks its legs.

When the small cat kicks, the large cat turns and watches.

The tiger is almost life-size, and measures 28 in (71 cm) tall and 70 in (178 cm) long.

Keys for playing tunes on the organ are behind a flap in the tiger's side.

MODERN DESCENDANTS

The Barecats is a modern wooden automaton designed by Paul Spooner. Turning a handle on its base makes the cats move. Spooner loves to get lifelike movement from simple mechanisms. As in its 16th-century ancestors, gear wheels transmit power, while cranks and cams (shaped rotors) create movement.

The beginnings of real robotics

THE RAPID DEVELOPMENT of electrical technology and electronics in the 20th century meant engineers could begin to build more sophisticated machines. These machines were hampered by their limited ability to handle information. They were not true robots, but gave a hint of things to come. As electronics continued to develop at an amazing pace, the simple circuits of pioneer devices evolved into elaborate computer-controlled systems. These would eventually lead to robots with enough intelligence to find their way around in the real world.

ELMER AND ELSIE

Grey Walter developed a robot tortoise with two amplifiers, a light sensor, a bump sensor, and two motors. It showed unexpectedly complex behavior. It seemed to explore its environment as most real animals do. Walter built the tortoise a mate and called the pair Elmer and Elsie. The idea of getting complex behavior from simple electronics is still being explored.

Photosensitive cells react to light given off by other tortoises.

A headlight attracts other tortoises.

A sensor detects when the case is rocked by bumping into something.

The motorized drive wheel allows the tortoise to change direction.

W. Grey Walter's robotic tortoise

Elektro

WORLD FIRST

W. Grey Walter was born in 1910 in Kansas City, MO, and educated in England. He was an expert in the usually separate fields of biology and electronics. In 1948, while working at the Burden Neurological Institute, Bristol, UK, Walter developed the first truly autonomous robot animal—a tortoise.

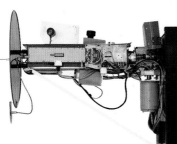

BIG BRAIN
The earliest programmable electronic computer was Eniac. It was built by US scientists Presper Eckert and John Mauchly in 1946. Computers now provide the brain power for most robots, but Eniac was not quite ready to fit inside a robot. It was a monster machine that barely fitted inside a room!

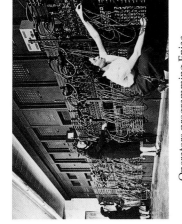

Operators programming Eniac

FREE WHEELING
Shakey was among the first robots to move freely without help. It was developed at the Stanford Research Institute in California between 1966 and 1972, and was the ancestor of today's Pioneer robots (pp. 24–25). Shakey was connected by radio to a computer. It worked—but the name tells you how well!

MOUSE MAN
In 1952, US engineer Claude Shannon built a robot mouse that could find its way around a metal maze using magnetic signals. The mouse was guided by data stored in circuits under the maze, and could quickly learn to navigate a new maze. It was one of the earliest experiments in artificial intelligence.

Modern maze-running robot

RODENT RACE
Maze-running mice are still used as learning tools in schools, and competitions form part of some college electronics courses. Today's mice have onboard computers, and the maze is usually just painted lines that the robots track using optical sensors. The mouse that navigates the maze fastest wins.

ONE MAN AND HIS DOG
Elektro, a 3D version of the imaginary robot of early fiction, came to life in 1939. This early humanoid was a star exhibit at the New York World's Fair. Elektro appeared with his electric dog Sparko, and his job was to give Mom, Pop, and the kids a vision of the future.

Sparko

Robots on the move

TRUE ROBOTS ARE able to move around to perform their designated tasks. Their motion needs to be more flexible and complex than other moving machines, such as cars, so they often require something more sophisticated than wheels. Arms and legs are one answer, but moving these effectively demands a robotic equivalent of muscles. Scientists and engineers have adapted existing power devices to create robot muscles. They have also invented new types of muscles. Some make innovative use of air pressure, while others are based on exotic metal alloys that shrink when heated.

Beam (Biology Electronics Aesthetics Mechanics) robotic butterfly

PRIME MOVER
Human muscles are natural motors that get their energy from glucose, a kind of sugar. Even the most advanced robot is a long way from being able to move like a human.

ALL WIRED UP
Muscle wire creates the movement of some miniature robots, like this solar-powered butterfly. Muscle wire is a mixture of nickel and titanium, called Nitinol. When heated by an electric current, the wire gets shorter and pulls with enough force to flap the robotic butterfly's lightweight wings.

CREEPY CRAWLERS
One way of making robots move is to have them imitate spiders or insects. These creatures have the advantage that, even if some of their legs are off the ground, they still have enough legs on the ground to keep their balance. Some roboticists are working on systems like this, despite the challenge involved in controlling so many legs.

Red-kneed tarantula

Robug III's top walking speed is 4 in (10 cm) per second.

Each leg is controlled by a separate microprocessor.

When the foot is placed on a surface, a pump in the leg draws air from under the foot to create a vacuum.

LOTS OF LEGS
Many robots need to travel over rough ground. The Robug team at Portsmouth University in the UK came up with the design for Robug III by studying the movements of crabs and spiders. This giant pneumatic, or air-powered, eight-legged robot can cope with almost anything. It can walk up walls and across ceilings, and can drag loads twice its own weight.

RO

Elma moves three legs at a time.

It always has three legs on the ground.

IMITATING INSECTS
Hexapod, or six-legged, robots like Elma can mimic the way insects move. Each leg, powered by its own computer-controlled electric motor, has to move in the right sequence, while adapting its action to the terrain. When Elma is switched on, it stands, limbers up, then sets off with jerky determination.

*Cybot is equipped
with an array
of sensors.*

*The hand can make
24 different powered
movements.*

THREE-WHEELER
Cybot, designed for *Real Robots* magazine,
uses wheels to get around. The wheels
limit it to traveling over smooth surfaces,
but offer the advantage of simpler
control. This frees up the robot's tiny
brain for more important tasks like
working out where to go next,
making it more independent.

Shadow
robotic arm

*The front wheel
can swivel,
which helps
with steering.*

PULLING POWER
Air muscles were invented in the
1950s for artificial limbs (p. 36), and
rediscovered by UK robot company
Shadow. Each air muscle is simply
a balloon inside a cylindrical net
cover. When inflated, the balloon
stretches the cover sideways,
making it shorter and creating
a pulling action. Air muscles are
relatively cheap and lightweight
compared to other pneumatic
systems used to move robots.

*These tubes link to an
air compressor, which
provides the power behind
Robug III's movements.*

*A whole group of muscles is
needed to move the fingers, as
in the human body.*

*The air muscles
in the forearm
connect to tubes
in the upper arm.*

*Most of Robug III's body is made
of light, strong carbon fiber.*

*Each leg has four
joints, which can
operate separately
or as a group.*

*It repeats the same
sequence over and
over again.*

*It can clamber over
uneven ground.*

*It leans forward to
help itself balance.*

Robot senses

To survive in the real world, robots need to be able to see, hear, feel, and tell where they are. Giving a robot the power to understand objects in the world around it is one of the most complex challenges of modern robotics. Machines already exist that can respond to touch, avoid bumping into things, react to sounds and smells, and even use senses, like sonar, that humans do not have. A robot that can sense as fully and reliably as a human, however, is still a long way off.

POWER GRIP
When people grip an object like a hammer, they curl their four fingers and thumb around it. They can exert great force, but cannot position or move the object precisely. Robot hands can mimic this power grip well.

The circuit board controls the motors.

Close-up model of human skin

The robotic hand cannot curl up as tightly as a human hand.

MECHANICAL MIMIC
Gripping strongly does not demand a refined sense of touch, which makes it easy for robots to copy. This robotic hand, designed for medical research at Reading University, UK, is able to mirror the position of the fingers and thumb used in the human power grip. It is driven by several small electric motors.

SENSITIVE ALL OVER
Robots cannot compete with the all-over sensitivity of animals, whose skin contains a dense network of sensitive nerve endings. These act as touch and bump sensors, and also detect heat or cold. In some animals, such as cats, long whiskers with nerve endings at their bases act as proximity, or nearness, sensors.

The fingers are jointed in the same places as human fingers.

The hand would be attached to an artificial arm.

EASY DOES IT
Gripping an object delicately is hard for a robot. The electronics that control the hand need feedback from sensors in the fingers. This is so that the motors can stop pushing as soon as they make contact with what they are gripping. Without this, the hand would either grip too weakly or crush the object.

EXPERT GRIP
The ability to grip delicately with the thumb and index finger has made humans expert tool-users. The full complexity of the human hand, with its elaborate system of sensors, nerves, and muscles, is only just beginning to be imitated in the robot world.

Rubbery pads on the fingertips help stop the pen from slipping.

The rubbery bumper contains bump sensors.

Pulses of infrared light emitted by the LEDs can be detected by the other robots in the group.

CLOSE ENCOUNTERS
Interactive robots that travel in groups need a range of senses. One of the most basic of these, touch, can be provided by a bumper. When the robot runs into something, the bumper makes an electrical contact that sends a signal to the robot's computer. The robot then backs off a little, changes direction, and moves on. Infrared signals allow robots in a group to communicate. Light-emitting diodes (LEDs) are used to release waves of infrared light that tell robots how close they are to each other.

FAR OR NEAR
This police officer is using a radar gun to detect how quickly cars are moving toward him. Some robots use similar technology to sense their distance from walls and other objects. They emit sound waves that bounce off objects, indicating their distance and speed of approach.

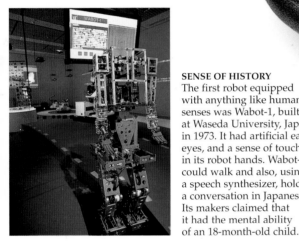

SENSE OF HISTORY
The first robot equipped with anything like human senses was Wabot-1, built at Waseda University, Japan, in 1973. It had artificial ears, eyes, and a sense of touch in its robot hands. Wabot-1 could walk and also, using a speech synthesizer, hold a conversation in Japanese. Its makers claimed that it had the mental ability of an 18-month-old child.

The LEDs form a circle so their light can be detected from all around.

This LED system is fully assembled and ready to be put to use.

LIGHT WORK
This image shows two circular circuit boards and a fully assembled LED system designed for an interactive group robot. With the LEDs in a ring and positioned on top of the robot, it is well-equipped for infrared communication.

ARTIFICIAL EYES
Real guide dogs use their sight to help their blind owners get around. The GuideCane detected objects using pulses of sound too high to hear. It was invented by Johann Borenstein at the University of Michigan. When it sensed something in its path, it steered its owner around the obstruction.

Three swarm robots designed for the Science Museum, London, UK

Artificial intelligence

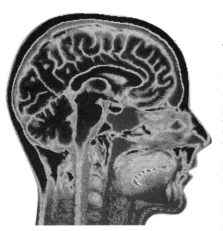

PEOPLE AND ANIMALS are intelligent. They can figure things out from incomplete information. A machine that could do this would have artificial intelligence (AI). Scientists have had some success with AI. For example, computers can now help doctors tell what is wrong with patients. Experts still do not agree, however, on whether a truly intelligent machine can be built, or how to build one. Complex computer programs have so far failed to provide robots with truly effective brains. It is now hoped that lots of small, simple programs can work together to create a really intelligent robot.

BRAIN POWER
The human brain has 100 billion nerve cells. These combine information from the outside world with stored memories to produce actions that help its owner survive. Other animal brains also do this, but only humans can master tasks as complex as speech and writing. Today's robot brains operate at the level of very simple animals.

Kasparov thinks out his next move.

Deep Blue displays its response on a screen.

INTELLIGENT FANTASY
This scene from Steven Spielberg's 2001 film *AI* shows David, a robot child, at an anti-robot rally called a Flesh Fair. David is programmed to form an unbreakable bond of love with a human mother. When abandoned, he begins a quest to become a real boy. Intelligent behavior like this is a long way from the capabilities of real robots.

CHESS CHAMP
On May 11, 1997, a chess-playing computer called Deep Blue forced world chess champion Garry Kasparov to resign from a game. It was the first time that a reigning world champion had lost to a computer under tournament conditions. Although Deep Blue had managed to outwit a human in an intellectual contest, it would not be able to answer the simple question "Do you like chess?"

COOL CALCULATOR
Designers are now trying to make ordinary home appliances a little brainier. Computers and sensors inside everyday gadgets allow them to make smart decisions. This refrigerator can not only bring the Internet right into the kitchen, but also help its busy user by coming up with ideas for meals based on the food currently stored in it.

"It's possible that our brains are too complicated to be understood by something as simple as our brains."

AARON SLOMAN
Professor of Artificial Intelligence, Birmingham University, UK

CLEVER COG

Cog is an attempt at a highly intelligent robot. The project was developed at the Massachusetts Institute of Technology as part of AI research. Cog can pinpoint the source of a noise, make eye contact with humans, and track a moving object. Cog's intelligence comes from many small computer programs working together, rather than a single large program.

Multiple video cameras give Cog stereoscopic, or three-dimensional, vision.

BABY BOT

Robot orangutan Lucy, created by Steve Grand, represents an animal that is less intelligent than an adult human. Grand's aim is for Lucy to learn in the way a human baby does. For example, Lucy will find out how to speak, use its arms, and interact with people.

Cog uses its hands to interact with real objects.

THAT'S LIFE

Artificial life researcher Mark Tilden designed this robot insect. He believes robots can evolve like natural organisms. This kind of AI coaxes complex behavior from simple components. The idea is used in computer programs that simulate nature to produce virtual creatures that learn, breed, and die.

Robots in industry

THE WORD "ROBOT" was originally used to describe factory workers, and that is just what the majority of real-life robots are. Unlike human workers, they have limitless energy, little intelligence, and no feelings. This makes them ideal for tiring, repetitive, or dangerous jobs. The earliest industrial robots simply helped ordinary machines by bringing them materials, or stacking the finished product. Many are still used in this way, but many more have become production machines in their own right, assembling cars or electronics, and even doing delicate jobs with plants or food. Although robots can not yet replace all human workers, they have made the world's factories much more productive.

Cables supply pneumatic power and electricity.

RURAL ROBOTS
This imaginary scene shows steam-driven robots cultivating farmland. In the 19th century, as industry attracted workers off the land and into factories, inventors began to dream of mechanizing farm work. Although today's farms are highly mechanized, they use special-purpose machines operated by human beings, not robots.

WELL WELDED
A robot-built car is a safer car, because robots never miss any of the thousands of welds it takes to assemble a car body. Today's cars are built on assembly lines, where rows of robots wield heavy welding guns in a shower of sparks. Because the robots cannot see, both the cars and the welding guns have to be positioned with great accuracy to ensure that all the welds come in the right place.

UX 120

Industrial welding robot

UNTOUCHED BY HAND
Sushi is now a popular dish outside its original home in Japan, and robots are helping to meet demand. This sushi robot can be reprogrammed to make many different varieties.

Humans can spread germs on hands, hair, and clothing.

HANDMADE SUSHI
Making sushi is a skilled job because customers like their sushi to look like a work of art. Strips of fish are combined with cooked rice, seasoned, and formed into rolls or balls. Hygiene is also important because the fish is served raw. This is where robots can make the greatest contribution.

Electrodes at the tip of the welding arm apply an electric current that fuses together pieces of metal.

1980s Unimate model

SEEDS OF THE FUTURE
This robot in a US agricultural lab is gently teasing out baby potato plants so that they can be put into individual pots. They will then produce seed potatoes, which will, in turn, produce crops of potatoes. Using robots in this way allows plant breeders to cultivate new varieties more quickly.

Robots welding cars on an assembly line

Unimate can be programmed to position parts with great accuracy.

FACTORY FIRST
The first industrial robot, Unimate, started work at General Motors in 1961. Unimate was originally designed to help make television picture tubes, but was used to stack hot metal parts. It followed step-by-step commands stored on a magnetic drum, and could lift about 2 tons. The robot was created by US engineers Joe Engelberger and George Devol.

Remote control

MANY OF TODAY'S robots are unable to make their own decisions. They would be helpless without a human sending them a constant stream of instructions by wire or radio. Strictly speaking, they are not robots at all, just machines that obey orders. Remote control is a way of getting around the problem of providing a machine with the knowledge and skill it needs to deal with the real world. It allows robots with little intelligence to do valuable jobs in science, industry, police work, medicine, and even archaeology.

DOMESTIC DUMMY
Omnibot 2000, launched in 1980 by the Tomy toy company, was an early domestic robot. It had little intelligence, so its owner had to use remote control to make the most of its limited capabilities. These included flashing its eyes, wheeling around, and opening and closing one gripper hand.

The disrupter fires blasts of water into the bomb to disarm it.

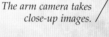

The arm camera takes close-up images.

Hobo's shotgun attachment can be used to gain access to buildings by shooting through doors.

From a safe distance

The Hobo remotely operated vehicle was developed in the 1980s to disarm terrorist bombs. It needed to be strong, reliable, and versatile to do its job. These qualities have since made it useful to the police, army, customs services, and private companies. Hobo gives its operator essential feedback through its built-in video cameras. It also comes with a range of attachments for various tasks.

Claw used to grab objects

Probe used to break windows

Disrupter used to disarm bombs

COMMAND AND CONTROL
Hobo is controlled through this tough, portable console, which transmits signals to the receiver mounted on the back of the robot. Using the pictures from Hobo's cameras, a bomb-disposal expert can move the robot, its arm, and its tools until the threat is neutralized.

Hobo's low center of gravity enables it to balance at steep angles.

ONWARD AND UPWARD
Hobo can go almost anywhere a human soldier could. Specially designed wheels and axles mean that curbs, steps, and bomb debris are no obstacle. It can turn in a small space and lift weights of 165 lb (75 kg). Hobo's advanced electronics stand up to rough handling, while its batteries are automatically managed to ensure that they do not go flat at a critical moment.

The drive camera is fixed in one position.

REALLY REMOTE
Robots can be controlled from almost any distance. *Sojourner*, part of the NASA Pathfinder mission, was the first robot to be controlled from Earth after landing on Mars. Because radio waves take seven minutes to get to Mars and back again, *Sojourner*'s controller could give only general instructions. For the detail, the robot was on its own and worked independently.

A speakerphone and video camera are located in the head.

NET EFFECT
CoWorker is the first off-the-shelf robot designed to be controlled via the Internet. Equipped with a camera and phone, it will trundle around factories and offices on command, allowing an expert to assess a situation or take part in a meeting without traveling to the site.

Souryu is equipped with a camera and microphone to help it locate survivors.

The rear video camera can be used to aim the shotgun.

FLEXIBLE FIND
Getting a camera into a pile of rubble to search for earthquake victims is a job for Souryu, which means "Blue Dragon." It is a remote-controlled, snakelike robot devised at the Tokyo Institute of Technology in Japan. The sections of its body can swivel independently to almost any angle, while its caterpillar treads can get a grip on even the rockiest surface.

Hobo's remote control unit receives messages from its operator.

CRATER NAVIGATOR
Dante 2 looked like a huge robotic spider. It had sensors in its legs that allowed them to operate automatically, but was also remote-controlled. In the summer of 1994, amid smoke and ash, it descended the crater of the Mount Spurr volcano in Antarctica on an experimental mission. Unfortunately, its legs buckled when it hit a rock, and the badly damaged robot had to be rescued by helicopter.

Each wheel is driven by a separate motor.

Ready-made robots

WHAT IF YOU HAVE an idea that demands a robot, but do not have the time or ability to design and make exactly what you need? An off-the-shelf model may be the answer. Today, ready-made robots come in various sizes, with accessories to adapt them for many purposes. They can be used for research, as exhibition guides, and in industry, where they carry products and documents around factories. Most of these machines are descendants of the first truly mobile robot, Shakey, completed in 1972, but are much smaller, lighter, and cheaper.

FACTORY FRIEND
Robot heavyweight Powerbot is an industrial successor to the Pioneer robots. It travels at 6 mph (10 km/h), carries 220 lb (100 kg), and is water-resistant. Powerbot can find its way around using its own intelligence, but it allows manual override. Uses include delivery, inspection, and surveillance.

READY-MADE FAMILY
Flakey was one of a line of mobile robots starting with Shakey and ending with today's ready-mades. It was developed by Kurt Konolige at the Stanford Research Institute. A heavyweight at 300 lb (140 kg), Flakey had two independently driven wheels, 12 sonar rangefinders, a video camera, and several onboard computers.

TEAM PLAYER
Designed for domestic chores and education, as well as professional research, Amigobot is based on Pioneer. Teachers like this robot's sturdy reliability and its versatile programming options. It is also designed to work in teams (pp. 56–57) with other Amigobots and can be adapted to play soccer.

CHEAP CHAMP
Pioneer I is a descendant of Flakey, via Erratic, a lower-cost research robot. Kurt Konolige developed Pioneer 1 as a commercial version of Erratic. The result was a robot that cost ten times less, and colleges could at last afford to teach robotics. Pioneer 1, fitted with soccer-playing accessories, won the RoboCup Soccer Championship in 1998. It was succeeded by Pioneer 2.

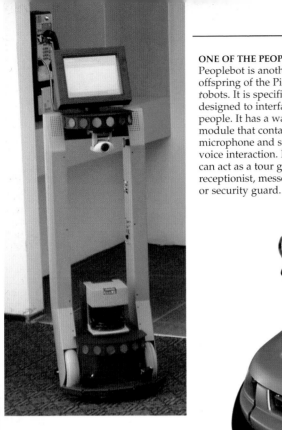

ONE OF THE PEOPLE
Peoplebot is another offspring of the Pioneer robots. It is specifically designed to interface with people. It has a waist-high module that contains a microphone and speakers for voice interaction. Peoplebot can act as a tour guide, receptionist, messenger, or security guard.

SMALL BUT CAPABLE
The Swiss-made Khepera, popular with experimenters and hobbyists, is perhaps the best-known ready-made robot. It measures only 2 in (55 mm) in diameter and weighs just 2 oz (70 g). Using the same software as other robots descended from Shakey, it is often a player in robot soccer games.

The cameras, which look like eyes on stalks, can tilt to get a panoramic view of the robot's surroundings.

BIG BROTHER
At 1 ft (30 cm) across, with six rugged wheels, Koala is Khepera's big brother and is capable of useful work. For example, it can clean floors with a vacuum cleaner when a special arm is attached. It is similar to Khepera, so any new ideas for it can be tried out on the smaller robot first.

A color camera takes snapshots of what the robot sees.

Accessories can be mounted on Amigobot's back.

The aerial receives messages from the radio control unit.

Amigobot is equipped with sonar sensors.

Robots in the classroom

WHEN YOU USE A computer at school, it is usually just a box on a table. However, some school computers have now sprouted wheels or legs and can roam around. They have become robots. Robots designed for classroom use are a fun way of learning basic math. They can also be used to introduce students to computer programming and help them discover how machines are controlled. Some classroom robots are used by young children, who enjoy this playful, interactive approach to learning. At a much higher level, in college courses, a classroom robot is essential for teaching the art and science of robotics to potential robot engineers of the future.

HIGH-TECH TEACHER
In the 1980s, a robot called Nutro, operated remotely by a human teacher, toured the US to teach children about the importance of a healthy diet. Real robots are not yet clever enough to do all the work of teachers themselves, but a remote-controlled one can make a lesson more memorable.

MATH TEACHER
South African mathematician Seymour Papert sparked interest in educational robots in the late 1960s. He had the idea of teaching children math by letting them play with a computer-controlled turtle that moved on a sheet of paper to draw shapes and patterns. He invented a simple but powerful programming language called Logo for the turtle.

Children program Roamer to follow a path

ROAM AROUND
Roamer is a round robot with concealed, motorized wheels. It can be programmed simply by pressing buttons on its cover, so it is popular in primary schools. Children can use Roamer to improve basic skills such as counting and telling left from right. The robot trundles around the classroom as instructed or moves a pen across paper to draw patterns. It can also play tunes. Teachers often encourage children to dress up their class robot as a pet or a monster.

TURTLE POWER
Turtle robots are now commonly used to introduce children to computer programming. This remote-controlled turtle, made by Valiant Technology, converts infrared signals from a computer into moves, turns, and pen action.

Roamer robot decorated with eyes

CLASS KIT

Rug Warrior is a small, intelligent mobile robot that can move around by itself. It comes as a kit that users have to assemble, and can easily be programmed from a PC, so is ideal for learning robotics. Rug Warrior is based on a robot developed for teaching robotics to university students. It is now one of the best-selling robot kits.

The plastic disc protects the electronics in case of a collision.

Rug Warrior prototype made to clean floors

SUMMER SCHOOL

The Carnegie Mellon University Mobile Robot Programming Lab runs summer courses for students interested in robotics. The students build and program mobile robots, which they are allowed to take home and keep when the course is over.

The links are the bones of the robot and the motors are its muscles.

Freddy's brain is a tiny computer programmed using a PC.

MIND GAMES

Freddy is a humanoid robot created using a kit called Lego Mindstorms. The kit allows children to design, build, program, and use their own robots. It was developed by Seymour Papert and Danish toy company Lego.

MISSING LINK

Robix construction kits are used to build robots that can walk, throw a ball, and even make a cup of tea. The kits are popular for teaching robotics and engineering at all levels, from high school to college. The kits consist of metal links that are joined with computer-controlled motors.

Playing with robots

THE IDEA OF A toy that appears to have a mind of its own would appeal to most children. Although early models were no more than plastic shapes with flashing lights, the latest toys can see, hear, and respond to commands from their owner, as well as exhibiting a range of emotions. Some even fall asleep at bedtime. Whatever the level of their abilities, designing robot toys is more than child's play for roboticists. It has provided them with a challenge to create better robots that can then be adapted for more serious purposes.

A green light flashes when the robot is switched on.

Early plastic, battery-powered toy robot

WALKIE-TALKIE
This 1950s toy robot was highly sophisticated for its time. It moved along, guided by a remote-control tether. It also showed the shape of things to come by being able to talk. But it was still a long way from being able to respond to human speech.

IT'S A WIND-UP
The first toy robots were often made from cheap printed metal, powered by clockwork, and wound up with a key. Toymakers had been producing moving figures using this method since the 19th century, but toys shaped like robots only became popular in the 1930s.

The legs are driven by an electric motor.

BATTERY BOT
By the 1960s, when cheap plastics, efficient electric motors, and good batteries had been developed, more sophisticated toy robots began to appear. The use of plastics allowed more elaborate body shapes, while battery power made it possible to add extras like flashing lights and beeping sounds.

FURRY FRIEND
Furby is a furry robotic creature with moving ears, eyes, and mouth. It can talk, sing, dance, and respond to its owner. It demands constant attention, but automatically sleeps when night falls. Furby was launched by toy designer Dave Hampton and Tiger Electronics in 1998 and was hugely popular.

A selection of the many Furby varieties

The speaker is located behind the switch on Furby's tummy.

The dog can obey basic commands.

Furby without its fur coat

Aibo playing with its ball

Aibo communicates by flashing colored lights on its head.

Two Aibo dogs interacting

Its behavior mimics that of a real dog.

PERFECT PETS
Sony's robotic dog, Aibo, is programmed with basic instincts to sleep, explore, exercise, and play. It can also express joy, sadness, anger, surprise, and fear using a combination of lights, sounds, and gestures. Aibo first went on sale in 1999. Since then, Sony has developed the toy to make it less expensive and more reliable. The latest models have an amazing range of abilities. They can even respond to the sound of their name and recognize their owner's face.

1999 ERS-110 Aibo model

"Toys like Aibo ... will come to populate our world more and more."

RODNEY BROOKS
Robot—The Future of Flesh and Machines

Battle of the bots

FIGHTING FOR FUN
Battling as entertainment has been popular since Roman times, when gladiators fought in arenas. Their fighting techniques are now copied by robots. Like gladiators, robot warriors need both strength and skill. The robots may have power-driven weapons and titanium armor, but humans still provide the skill—by remote control.

THE MACHINES ENTER the arena. Engines roar and metal flies. The battlebots are in action, and the crowd goes wild. The challenge is to design and build a remote-controlled machine (not a true robot) that can travel quickly and reliably over a wide area and outdo the others in strength and agility. It can be dangerous if you don't know what you're doing, but is great fun both to compete in and to watch. Many serious robot engineers regard combat robotics as a way of improving their skills. It is a rewarding and fun way of developing the components that are also part of more practical, everyday robots.

Repairs may be needed between competition rounds.

WARRIORS GREAT AND SMALL
Combat robot contestants are divided into classes according to their weight to ensure fair fights. This competitor is working on a robot for a lightweight class. The classes range from monsters weighing 390 lb (177 kg) to sozbots, or sixteen-ounce robots, which weigh less than 1 lb (0.5 kg). There are also restrictions on the size of the robots and the weapons they carry. Explosives are not allowed!

IN IT FROM THE START
One of the first robot combat events was BotBash, which started as two robots fighting in a chalk circle—much simpler than this recent BotBash arena. Today, events are organized by groups all over the world. Most follow rules laid down by the US Robot Fighting League.

The armored shell is made from light but tough fiberglass matting.

Matilda's tusk weapons are powered by hydraulics.

Building a battle robot

The challenge of finding solutions to technical problems is as interesting to many combat robot builders as the actual battles. British robot team Shredder is typical. It uses careful design and precision engineering to turn basic ideas into successful robotic fighting machines. Any failure is immediate and obvious— electrics may fail, motors may burn out, or armor may not withstand attack, so the learning curve is steep. But lessons learned the hard way can be put to use in other projects.

Weapon

Wheel

Batteries

Shredder is controlled by an adapted model aircraft remote-control console.

1 VIRTUAL ROBOT
The Shredder team first considers the weight of the components, what materials to use, how much power is required, and where to put the large batteries that will supply this. The team uses a computer to plan the design of their robot.

3 INTO BATTLE
The final challenge is to test the robot in battle. It has no intelligence of its own, but relies on radio signals from its driver. It takes a lot of skill to win a fight. The remote-control unit works a bit like a video game console. One thumb makes the robot move, while the other operates the weapons.

The body is made of light, strong titanium.

The wheels are solid, not air-filled, to avoid punctures.

Each disc has two cutting teeth.

2 BUILDING THE BOT
A team member bolts on the robot's cutting discs, which rotate in opposite directions. The teeth on the edge of the discs are designed to cut through the tough armor of other battlebots. This is just part of the long and painstaking building process.

Two powerful lifting arms act as weapons.

Dreadnaut has a low ground clearance to prevent other robots from flipping it over.

TV SPECTACULARS
Robot Wars is a television show in which robots built by competitors, like Dreadnaut, do battle with each other and with the show's resident robots, including dinosaur-like Matilda. Other fearsome resident robots are Shunt, which carries an ax that can cut opponents in half, and Dead Metal, which has pneumatic pincers and a circular saw. Battling robots make great TV!

Sporting robots

19th-century illustration showing a steam-powered robot baseball pitcher

THERE IS much to learn—and lots of fun to be had—building robots to play human sports. Robots already compete in simplified games, but matching the speed and skill of a human is proving to be a much tougher task. It is a worthwhile goal, though, because building a successful player will teach roboticists how to design better robots for everyday use. Today, a robot can walk across a field and kick a ball into an open goal. When it can run toward a goal defended by humans, and still score, the robot age will be here.

Humanoid robot SDR-3X dribbling a soccer ball

The robot's body position mimics that of the human player.

Soccer star Mia Hamm dribbling a ball

LONG-TERM GOAL
RoboCup is a project that aims to develop a team of robots to beat the human world soccer champions by 2050. The robots will have to mimic the smooth, balanced movements of a human player, seen in skills such as dribbling, and use these intelligently. More than 3,000 people in 35 countries are working on RoboCup projects.

The control panel can be used to select various game programs.

On-Off
A
B
Run   Prgn

Lego soccer-playing robots designed by cybernetics students

The raised kicking arm will flick the ball away from the other robot.

The robot is moving in to try to take the ball.

SIMPLE SOCCER
The game of soccer has been reduced to its bare essentials to allow for the limited capabilities of low-cost, experimental robots. A robot team can consist of just one player. The robot simply has to gain possession of the ball and get it into the opponent's goal. Most soccer-playing robots navigate using infrared sensors. They have tiny brains, and cannot see well, so games are often abandoned when both teams get lost!

WORLD CLASS
More than 60 teams competed in the 1998 Robot Soccer World Cup in Paris, France. The robots played 20-minute matches without human help, controlled by on-board or remote computers and sensors. Since 2002, the competition has included humanoid robots. They cannot yet play games, but some can dribble and pass balls, and even score goals.

Robot Sumo competition, Japan, 1992

Robot Soccer World Cup, 1998

Soccer-playing robots passing the ball

GETTING PUSHY
In Robot Sumo, two robots wrestle in a ring 5 ft (154 cm) across. Unlike battlebots, which are armed, they rely on strength and skill alone. The bout ends when one robot is pushed out of the ring or breaks down. Sumo robots can be autonomous, with an onboard computer, or controlled from the ringside.

The robots are powered by batteries housed near the control panel.

Soccer-playing robots about to clash in a struggle for possession of the ball

The ball is light and large to make the game easier.

RCX 1.0

The ball emits infrared signals so that the robots can locate it.

The wheels are designed to work on smooth, flat surfaces.

The robot maneuvers the ball using a curved gripper bar.

Robots in the lab

SCIENTIFIC RESEARCH depends heavily on laboratory work where the same painstaking but tedious procedure has to be repeated over and over again. This is exactly what robots are good at. They do not get bored and their actions never vary, so they can do repetitive chores without making mistakes. Robots are ideal for work like developing new drugs, which requires a huge number of tests to be repeated without any random variations. They are also immune to germs, radioactivity, and chemicals, so can do things that are too risky for humans.

The operator programs the robotic arm from outside the clean room.

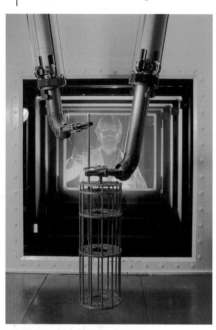

AT ARM'S LENGTH
The first laboratory robots were arms like these. They were connected mechanically to their human operator, whose movements they copied directly. They were used for remote handling of hazardous materials in the nuclear industry. Newer arms are electrically powered and connected to their operator via electronic control systems.

ROBOT TECHNICIAN
The simplest type of laboratory robot is a fixed arm. If everything is within reach, it can measure out liquids, stack specimens, and so on. A robot like this, controlled by a computer, can pick up and place things where needed as well as supply chemical measuring devices with samples for analysis.

UMI
RTX

UMI
RTX

The fixed arm has a smooth tipping action.

The protective suit is an extra guard against contamination.

All windows and doors are sealed to prevent airborne particles from entering the clean room.

The arm can mix, pour, and sort substances.

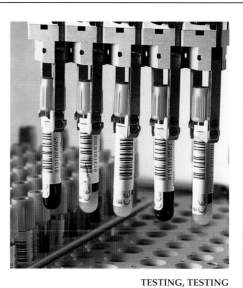

TESTING, TESTING
When a doctor sends blood to the lab for tests, the sample is often handled by a robot. Thousands of specimen tubes flood into clinical laboratories every day, and a robot can keep track of them all. In one hour the robot may pick up 2,000 tubes, read their labels, and put them in the right rack for the tests they need.

GROWING CELLS
SelecT is an automatic cell-culturing machine used in biomedical research. This involves growing cells in laboratory glassware for developing medicines, biological compounds, and gene therapy. SelecT was designed with the help of major drug companies. It improves on the speed, accuracy, and consistency of manual methods.

Cell cultures growing in petri dishes

The arm is fixed, so everything it needs must be placed within its reach.

Robots in medicine

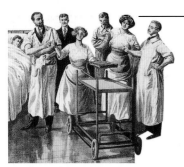

TWENTY YEARS AGO it would have been unthinkable to let a robot loose in an operating room. But with today's more powerful computers and improved mechanical techniques, it is possible for a closely supervised robot to wield the knife in a number of critical procedures. Human doctors remain in control, of course, but in another 20 years the face of medicine may look very different. Robotics also promises to revolutionize artificial limbs. Knowledge gained during research into walking robots is now being used to develop ways of helping people with spinal injuries recover movement in their legs.

X-rays of the patient's chest provide additional guidance.

ELECTRIC FINGERS
People unfortunate enough to lose an arm once had little choice but to accept a rigid replacement with an ineffective, hooklike hand. With technology derived partly from robotics research, things are improving. Patients may now have an electric hand with battery-powered fingers that move in response to the movements of muscles in the remaining part of their arm.

Modern artificial hand showing internal mechanics

A patient's meal is delivered from Helpmate's hatch.

The surgeon views a 3D image of the operation site and controls the robot arms.

EMERGENCY STOP

GOPHER

GOPHER

HelpMate

TRC

HOSPITAL HELPER
Helpmate is a robot designed for use in hospitals. It is a mechanical porter that carries meals, specimens, drugs, records, and X-rays back and forth between different parts of the hospital. Helpmate can find its way through hallways and use elevators. Built-in safety devices stop it from running into the patients.

SMART HEART SURGERY
In 2002, US surgeon Michael Argenziano used a robot called DaVinci to repair heart defects that would normally require the patient's chest to be opened up. Using DaVinci, Argenziano made the repairs through four holes, each just 0.5 in (1 cm) wide. The procedure was successful for 14 out of 15 patients. They were ready to go home after three days instead of the usual seven.

A close-up view of the operation guides the surgeon.

SPREADING SKILLS

The first long-distance operation, when a surgeon in one country operated on a patient in another, was performed in 2001. The patient was in France and the surgeons were in New York. A live video link allowed them to manipulate robot arms 3,000 miles (4,800 km) away. The robot even understood speech commands such as "up" or "down." This technology makes surgeons' skills more widely available.

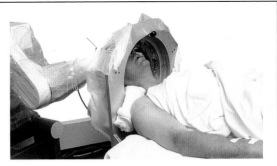

PRECISION BRAINWORK

NeuroMate is the first robotic system developed specifically for a type of brain surgery in which instruments are positioned precisely before being used. It reduces operating time by allowing surgeons to plan procedures in advance. NeuroMate also shows the surgeons what is going on during the operation, so that they can stay in control.

Powerful lighting is needed, as in all surgery.

Live images of the operation site are shown on the screen.

A number of robot arms work together on the patient.

The patient is anesthetized and must be kept very still.

Helping around the home

AT LONG LAST, engineers are building robots that are capable of helping with some of the boring chores that fill our lives. We do not yet have a robot that can do the ironing or take out the garbage, but domestic robots can now clean the floor or mow the lawn while we do more interesting things. Floors and lawns are fairly simple spaces. Progress in the complicated, three-dimensional environment of an entire home has been much slower. Tasks that seem easy to us, like climbing stairs or sorting trash from prized possessions, present a real challenge to robots. It looks as if people will have to do most of their own chores for years to come.

1929 illustration from *Le Petit Inventeur* showing the servant of the future cleaning its master's shoes

Wakamaru sees the world through two cameras.

GUARD DRAGON
Banryu, whose name means "guard dragon," can walk at 50 ft (15 m) a minute and step over a 6-in (15-cm) threshold. It can smell burning, see, and hear. If Banryu detects danger, it reports by cell phone to its owner, who can control it remotely.

TALKATIVE TECHNOLOGY
Wakamaru is the first robot designed with the care of elderly people in mind. It transmits pictures of its owner to watching relatives using a built-in cell phone and webcam. It also knows 10,000 words, so it can talk well. If its owner remains quiet for a set length of time, Wakamaru asks, "Are you all right?" and, if necessary, calls emergency services.

AHEAD OF ITS TIME
US company Androbot launched Topo, a toylike plastic robot, in 1983. Nolan Bushnell, Topo's designer, saw it as a helpful friend rather than a servant. The 3-ft (90-cm) robot was controlled by a PC via a radio link. Topo is now a sought-after antique.

CLEVER CLEANER

Launched in 2001, the Electrolux Trilobite was one of the first domestic robots to go on sale. It is simply an intelligent version of a traditional vacuum cleaner. The Trilobite navigates using ultrasound, and magnetic strips across doorways stop it from wandering off. It cleans without help for an hour, then returns to its battery charger.

WISHFUL THINKING

This imaginary robot from 1927 is doing the work of a valet, whose job is to care for clothes. After World War I, wealthy people found it hard to get domestic servants, which promoted interest in labor-saving gadgets.

The five keys can be used to control the robot.

ON GUARD!

Japanese guard robot Maron-1, made by Fujitsu, is 14 in (36 cm) tall and runs on wheels. It has a built-in cell phone so that it can take instructions from its owner, and sensors to detect movement. If someone breaks in when Maron-1 is on guard, it sounds an alarm and phones its owner, who can see what is going on through Maron's two rotating camera eyes.

MAGIC MOWER

Robomow is one of a number of robot lawnmowers that have appeared over the last few years. Powered by a rechargeable battery, it mows the lawn without human help. A wire buried around the lawn's edge keeps the robot on the grass, while bump and lift sensors stop it from giving the family pet a haircut!

Going where it's hard to go

ROBOTS ARE ideal for situations where human operators would be exposed to danger, could not actually reach the work, or would find the job so tedious or unpleasant that they would not do it well. In these cases, the typical robot's nonhuman shape is a distinct advantage—feet that grip walls like a lizard, wheels that can steer through slimy pipes, or a body that can tolerate huge doses of radiation make these adventurous automata indispensable. Robots are hard at work as window-cleaners, sewer inspectors, and even firefighters, leaving humans free to undertake less risky and unpleasant tasks.

MINI MIMIC

US company iRobot is working on a miniature robot that mimics the gecko lizard. The robot should be able to climb walls that defeat larger machines. Its multiple legs will probably have claws for soft surfaces and sticky pads for harder ones, just like a real gecko. Jobs for the robot could include surveillance and mine detection.

Tokay gecko

The body is jointed in the middle, which allows Robug II to move from vertical to horizontal surfaces, and vice versa.

The movement of each limb is controlled by a microprocessor.

Pneumatic cylinders power the limbs.

Vacuum suction grippers are located on the underside of each foot.

NUCLEAR EXPLORER

Climbing walls to aid the inspection of nuclear power plants is all in a day's work for Robug II. It is one of a series of spider-like robots developed by UK company Portech. Robug II moves in stages, resting between steps to seek out fresh footholds. Vacuum suckers on the robot's feet enable it to scale almost any surface. Extra suckers underneath the body lock it onto the surface to give a stable working position once it has climbed to the right spot. Its brain is a PC, connected by a cable.

WINDOW WALKER

Wall-climbing robots have obvious uses for jobs such as cleaning large buildings, where it is difficult to provide access for humans. The Ninja series of four-legged climbers was developed at the Tokyo Institute of Technology in Japan from 1990 onward. Despite their clumsy appearance, the robots can climb walls at 25 ft (7.5 m) per minute.

DOWN THE TUBES

Kurt is a German sewer-inspection robot. Sewers are often inspected by remote-controlled robots, but the control cables can get tangled on tight bends. Kurt doesn't need a cable because it has enough intelligence to follow every twist on its own. Using a digital map of the system and a set of known landmarks, it can find its way to any given point to gather information on the state of the pipes.

The robot reports any pipes in need of repair and any blockages.

Twin lasers guide Kurt through the sewer pipes.

The camera relays images to the person operating the robot.

ART WORK

Most visitors to Paris, France, know the glass pyramid outside the Louvre art gallery. But few will have realized how it is kept clean. Following earlier experiments, seen here, the pyramid is now cleaned by a robot built specially for the job by inventor Henry Seemann. The robot climbs using three large sucker feet and delivers pressurized cleaning solution.

Robin can seal radioactive waste in containers, making it safer for humans to handle and dispose of.

FIREFIGHTER

If fire breaks out in a nuclear or chemical plant, a Telerob MV4 may be needed. The robot can be operated at a safe distance by someone watching a television screen, and can douse flames without endangering life.

RESISTING RADIATION

Robin the robot was designed for use in the nuclear industry. Robots are used in parts of this industry because they are unaffected by levels of radioactivity that would kill human workers. Robin's four legs can step over obstacles, enabling it to move nuclear material around in a workplace that may be cluttered with cables and pipes.

Caterpillar treads make light work of uneven ground.

Flying and driving

IMAGINE A ROBOT car that could whiz you through the traffic to anywhere you wanted. Unfortunately, despite years of research, basic driving skills that most humans can learn remain beyond the reach of robots. The race to build a car that can drive itself is still on. High above the roads, however, where there are fewer things to bump into, great progress has been made. Pilotless planes of all sizes now fly the skies to make measurements, take pictures, or relay radio signals.

AUTO PILOT
Pathfinder is a pilotless airplane that is driven by solar-powered electric motors. It was developed by US company AeroVironment in 1971. Pathfinder-plus, a later version, has flown to 82,000 ft (25,000 m).

GIANT MODEL
Pilotless planes are now in regular use for surveillance. One of the most successful, Aerosonde, comes from Australia. It made its first independent flight in 1997, and the following year crossed the Atlantic Ocean. With its 10-ft (3-m) wingspan and 24cc engine, Aerosonde is rather like a giant model aircraft. After launching from a car roof rack, it navigates using the Global Positioning System (GPS).

The streamlined cooling houses the electronics.

A pressure tube measures the plane's speed.

A DAY'S WORK
Aerosonde has many uses. Here, its shadow crosses desert terrain as it collects meteorological, or weather-forecasting, data. It can also monitor traffic congestion or spy on illegal activities. It flies regularly in Alaska to measure the temperature of the sea ice. In 2003, Aerosonde was deployed during peacekeeping operations in the Solomon Islands in the South Pacific Ocean.

BIGGER AND BETTER
Pathfinder's successor Helios is larger and can fly higher. In 2001, it broke the world altitude record. It navigates using GPS. Later models will be able to fly by night as well as day, offering serious competition to communications satellites.

A graphite tailboom supports the tail.

The fiberglass tail stabilizes the plane.

SERIOUS SNAPS
Global Hawk is a US military robot plane that can provide continuous images of a battlefield. Its development began in 1995. By 2002, it was being used in Afghanistan. It produced more than 15,000 high-resolution images.

Long, narrow wings help to reduce drag.

aerosonde

AEROSONDE ROBOTIC AIRCRAFT

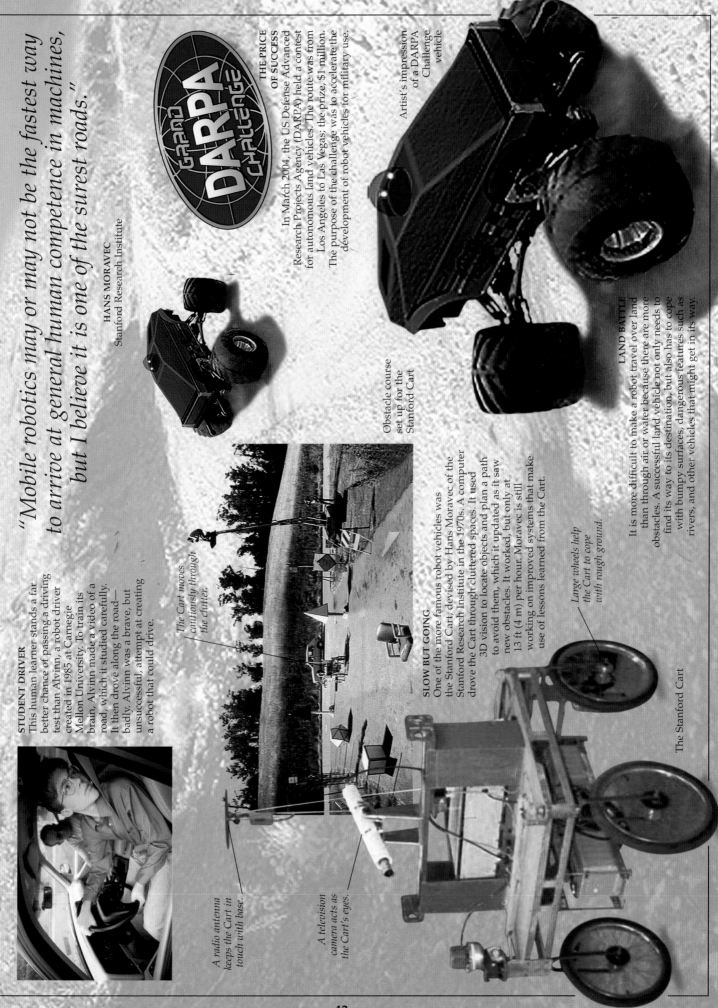

"Mobile robotics may or may not be the fastest way to arrive at general human competence in machines, but I believe it is one of the surest roads."

HANS MORAVEC
Stanford Research Institute

THE PRICE OF SUCCESS
In March 2004, the US Defense Advanced Research Projects Agency (DARPA) held a contest for autonomous land vehicles. The route was from Los Angeles to Las Vegas; the prize, $1 million. The purpose of the challenge was to accelerate the development of robot vehicles for military use.

Artist's impression of a DARPA Challenge vehicle

LAND BATTLE
It is more difficult to make a robot travel over land than through air or water because there are more obstacles. A successful land vehicle not only needs to find its way to its destination, but also has to cope with bumpy surfaces, dangerous features such as rivers, and other vehicles that might get in its way.

STUDENT DRIVER
This human learner stands a far better chance of passing a driving test than Alvinn, a robot driver created in 1985 at Carnegie Mellon University. To train its brain, Alvinn made a video of a road, which it studied carefully. It then drove along the road—badly. Alvinn was a brave, but unsuccessful, attempt at creating a robot that could drive.

Obstacle course set up for the Stanford Cart

The Cart moves cautiously through the clutter.

SLOW BUT GOING
One of the more famous robot vehicles was the Stanford Cart, devised by Hans Moravec of the Stanford Research Institute in the 1970s. A computer drove the Cart through cluttered spaces. It used 3D vision to locate objects and plan a path to avoid them, which it updated as it saw new obstacles. It worked, but only at 13 ft (4 m) per hour. Moravec is still working on improved systems that make use of lessons learned from the Cart.

Large wheels help the Cart to cope with rough ground.

A radio antenna keeps the Cart in touch with base.

A television camera acts as the Cart's eyes.

The Stanford Cart

43

Underwater robots

TWO-THIRDS OF OUR planet is covered by water, and most of this watery world is unexplored. Robots are now an essential tool for ocean explorers. Some are remote-controlled vehicles towed behind ships. Others are miniature submarines carrying a human crew but equipped with robot arms. However, many are fully autonomous. They can navigate to a given point and automatically carry out a survey using video, sonar, or other devices. Even the best of today's underwater robots, though, are crude compared with the sea creatures they meet. The latest research imitates the abilities of these creatures, giving the robots improved intelligence, speed, and endurance.

The fiberglass body is jointed to allow Roboshark to swim.

CAMERA SHARK
Filming sharks without disturbing their natural behavior was hard until Roboshark came along. Designed for a British television network, the BBC, the fiberglass fish is programmed to swim among real sharks, carrying a TV camera to catch them in action. Roboshark is based on a Pacific gray reef shark. It is 6 ft 6 in (2 m) long and can swim at 3 mph (5 km/h). This model is remote-controlled, but roboticists hope that a later version will make its own decisions.

Stretch fabric covers the robotic fish.

The springy body is full of complex moving parts.

SHIPWRECK AHOY
One of the main uses of undersea robots is to explore the sea floor. True autonomous underwater vehicles (AUVs) navigate independently over long distances, returning with recorded data. Others are controlled from ships on the surface. Here, a shipwreck is under investigation by Hyball. A cable supplies power and control for the robot and carries pictures of the wreck to the surface. Powerful lights are needed, because it is completely dark at depths below about 330 ft (100 m).

EFFICIENT FISH
How do fish glide so smoothly through the water? John Kumph of the Massachusetts Institute of Technology has created a robot fish that may help to answer the question. Its body, a fiberglass spring covered with Lycra, flips and turns in the water as easily as a real fish.

Electric thrusters move the robot around.

BEACH BABY
Ariel is a robot crab that may soon be used to clear mines from seashore minefields. Walking just like a crab, Ariel can scramble over obstacles and crevices that would defeat a wheeled robot. Even if it gets flipped over by a wave, Aerial simply keeps on walking—upside down!

EXPERIENCED EXPLORER

Autosub, an AUV developed in the UK, is an independent robot submarine that has completed more than 200 scientific missions. These include observing herring in the North Sea and locating valuable metals on the floor of a Scottish lake. Autosub has even been to Antarctica, where it dove beneath the ice of the Weddell Sea.

A conventional robot arm supports the Elephant's Trunk.

UNDERWATER ACTION

Ordinary robot arms have problems under the sea. Positioning them accurately is time-consuming, and their movements stir up sediment, obscuring vision. A new type of arm, developed at Heriot-Watt University in Scotland, has flexible rubber sections moved by air instead of metal parts. The principle of this Parallel Bellows Actuator (nicknamed the Elephant's Trunk) could also be used to propel a submarine equipped with flexing fins.

TREASURE HUNTER

The French submarine *Nautile* is not a robot. It has a three-person crew—pilot, co-pilot, and observer—who work in a compartment only 7 ft (2.1 m) in diameter. *Nautile* does, however, have a robot arm and can even launch its own little remote-controlled sub. As one of the few submarines that can operate at a depth of 3.5 miles (6,000 m), it was used to recover treasures from the wreck of the *Titanic*, which sank in the North Atlantic in 1912.

All the equipment is mounted on an internal frame.

Part of the ship's equipment is retrieved by the arm.

Cables convey signals to computers.

SUPER SUBMARINES

Every year, a number of US colleges compete to build the fastest, most intelligent robot sub. Operating entirely under their own control, the robots look for bar-coded boxes in a deep pool. They have to decipher the code on each box, measure its depth, and report this back to base. In 2002, Cornell University's AUV, seen here, came second. It found one more box than the winner, but took longer.

Robots in space

SPACE IS A HOSTILE environment. There is no air and, with little or no atmosphere for protection, everything gets very hot when the sun shines and very cold when it doesn't. Robots can handle these conditions much better than astronauts can. They are also cheaper to operate, because they require no life-support system and can be left behind after a mission. Everything they have found out can simply be sent back to Earth by radio. But robots that explore remote planets such as Mars need a lot of intelligence. Remote control is not possible because instructions from Earth take several minutes to reach them. Once they have landed, they are on their own.

The spacewalker uses the arm to steady himself.

Joints in the arm make it flexible.

Canada

STRONG ARM
This robot arm is an important part of the International Space Station. Repairing or modifying the outside of the station is difficult because the slightest push on a tool sends its user spinning backward. The arm, controlled from inside the station, is used to carry materials to where they are needed, as well as to steady or tether spacewalkers.

PICTURE THAT
Aercam Sprint is a free-flying robot TV camera. The basketball-like camera was first released during a 1997 Shuttle flight. Since this early model could easily have failed, it only flew around inside the Shuttle, remotely controlled by pilot Steve Lindsey. Future versions of the flying camera may not need remote control.

Solar panels lined the inside of the lander's lid.

The lander had eight wheels.

The camera is protected from collisions with other equipment by the cushioned surface.

MOON WANDERER
In 1970, the Russian explorer *Lunokhod* became the first robot to land on the Moon. Lunokhod weighed more than 1,650 lb (750 kg) on Earth. The solar-powered vehicle, maneuvered by a team on Earth, took 20,000 photographs and sent back data from 500 lunar soil samples.

The entomopter comes in to land on its refueling platform.

SPACE SPIDER

NASA researchers have created Spider-bot, a six-legged micro-robot that may one day explore remote planets. Unlike wheeled rovers, a robot with legs can cope with rocky and furrowed terrain. The prototype fits in the palm of the hand. Future versions could be even smaller.

IN A FLAP

Scientists are currently working on an entomopter, or robot insect, that they think could one day fly on Mars. Because of the thin atmosphere on Mars, a fixed-wing plane would have to travel at more than 250 mph (400 km/h) to stay airborne, making exploration difficult. An entomopter could move slowly on flapping wings, studying the landscape from the air and landing to collect samples.

The long neck gives the rover a good vantage point.

Four cameras are positioned at the top of the rover's neck.

THE BEAGLE HAS LANDED

Beagle 2 was launched on board the European Space Agency's flight to Mars in June 2003. Designed at the Open University, *Beagle 2*'s mission is to seek life on the Red Planet. The solar-powered robot is autonomous, but also responds to remote control. Its flexible arm carries a range of instruments and cameras.

SPIRIT AND OPPORTUNITY

The latest Mars rovers, *Spirit* and *Opportunity*, were launched in June and July of 2003 and scheduled to land in January 2004. The two robots are identical, but will explore different regions. They will be able to travel 330 ft (100 m) in a Martian day (24 hr 40 min)—almost as far as the first US Mars rover, *Sojourner*, did in its entire life. More robot rovers designed to study Mars and try out new landing technology may be launched as early as 2007.

Solar panels on top of the body provide power.

Robots and art

PAINTING A PICTURE seems like a uniquely human activity, but it is not. Some robots can do it. They may either use a television camera as an eye to look at someone and draw their portrait, or recall images stored in a computer memory to create a picture from their robot imagination. Perhaps because of this, some human artists have given up painting pictures and taken to building robots. Some weld together junk parts to build amusing robotlike sculptures. Others build real robots that are programmed to put on artistic performances ranging from the poetic to the downright scary.

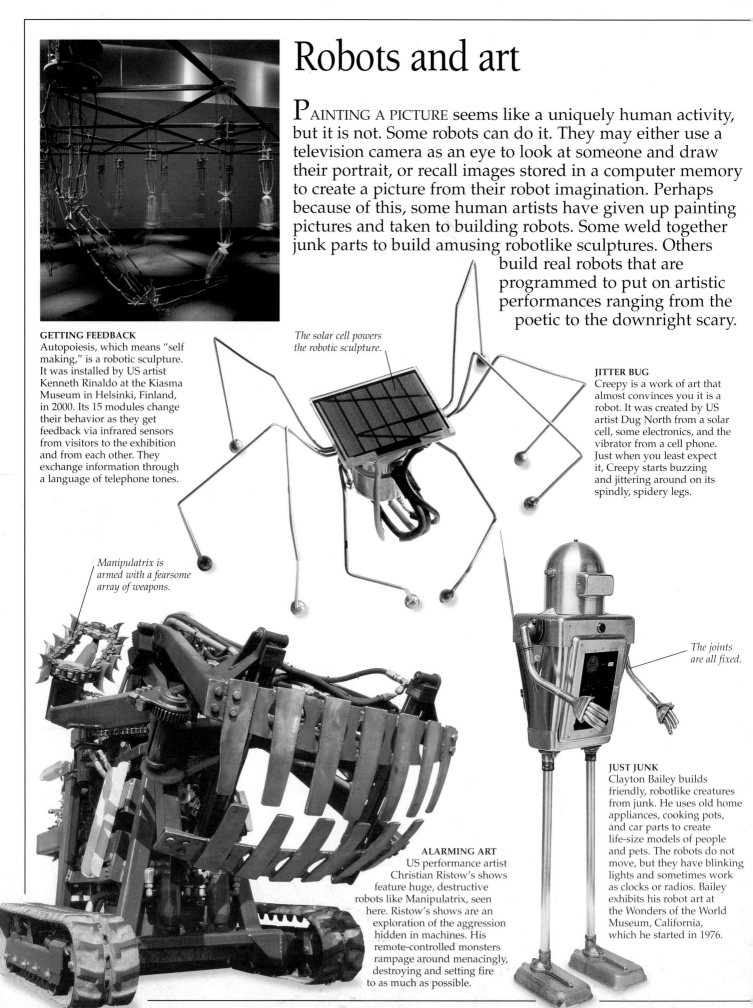

GETTING FEEDBACK
Autopoiesis, which means "self making," is a robotic sculpture. It was installed by US artist Kenneth Rinaldo at the Kiasma Museum in Helsinki, Finland, in 2000. Its 15 modules change their behavior as they get feedback via infrared sensors from visitors to the exhibition and from each other. They exchange information through a language of telephone tones.

The solar cell powers the robotic sculpture.

JITTER BUG
Creepy is a work of art that almost convinces you it is a robot. It was created by US artist Dug North from a solar cell, some electronics, and the vibrator from a cell phone. Just when you least expect it, Creepy starts buzzing and jittering around on its spindly, spidery legs.

Manipulatrix is armed with a fearsome array of weapons.

The joints are all fixed.

ALARMING ART
US performance artist Christian Ristow's shows feature huge, destructive robots like Manipulatrix, seen here. Ristow's shows are an exploration of the aggression hidden in machines. His remote-controlled monsters rampage around menacingly, destroying and setting fire to as much as possible.

JUST JUNK
Clayton Bailey builds friendly, robotlike creatures from junk. He uses old home appliances, cooking pots, and car parts to create life-size models of people and pets. The robots do not move, but they have blinking lights and sometimes work as clocks or radios. Bailey exhibits his robot art at the Wonders of the World Museum, California, which he started in 1976.

Aaron mixes paints to the exact color required.

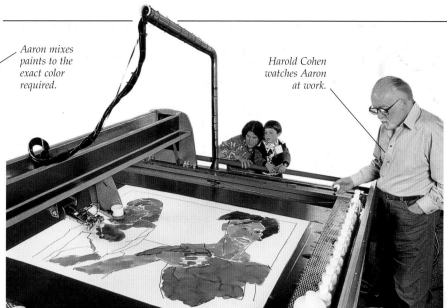

Harold Cohen watches Aaron at work.

ROBOT REALIST
Aaron is not a true robot, but a computer connected to a large drawing machine. British artist Harold Cohen has been working on Aaron since 1973. It makes several original sketches, Cohen selects one, then Aaron paints the final picture. Its paintings have been hung in several art galleries.

The arm is jointed to allow a full range of movement.

ARTISTIC TEMPERAMENT
The German group Robotlab aims to increase people's awareness of robots. The group demonstrates its portrait-painting robot, a standard Kuka industrial arm, in public places. The robot, equipped with TV camera vision and special software, draws portraits that are usually a good likeness. As soon as a drawing is finished, though, the robot rubs it out in a gesture of defiance.

The camera is positioned on top of the drawing arm.

The robot is bolted to the floor, just as it would be in industry.

A robot's-eye view of the work in progress

A boy sits to have his portrait drawn by a Robotlab industrial arm

Musical robots

PLAYING A MUSICAL instrument demands a combination of movement and senses that presents a real challenge to robot engineers. Music has to be played with feeling, not just mechanically. Despite this, sophisticated robot pianos and other automatic instruments were available as long ago as the early 20th century. Some of the first tests of modern robots involved music, precisely because playing an instrument requires such careful coordination. Musical robots have not yet replaced human musicians, but they have put a few drummers out of a job. Drum machines controlled by computers now underpin the backing tracks of much popular music.

RECORD PLAYERS
Robot bands were popular in Paris, France, in the 1950s. They were not real robots, but simply moved in time to music from a gramophone record. This trio was created by French inventor Didier Jouas-Poutrel in 1958. It could play any tune the dancers requested—as long as the record was available.

The paper is punched as the musician plays.

ROLL MODEL
In the 1920s, robot pianos brought "live" music into some homes. Musicians played on a recording piano that captured their actions as holes in a paper roll. This was played back on a reproducing piano that repeated every detail of the performance.

Mubot plays an ordinary violin.

The violinist from the Mubot trio

VIRTUAL VIRTUOSO
Mubot was a set of robots that could play a real recorder, violin, and cello. Japanese engineer Makoto Kajitani started work on the project in the late 1980s. His idea was not only to produce a robotic trio, but also to improve his expertise by studying a difficult problem. Kajitani also thought that Mubot would be a useful tool for scientists studying musical instruments.

The flute needs no modification.

It has realistic fingertips.

WF3-RIX plays with a human flutist

WF3-RIX playing a flute

CUTE FLUTE
Atsuo Takanishi of Waseda University believes that music, with its combination of mechanical and emotional demands, can help us find out what it takes to build a better humanoid robot. His robot flutist WF3-RIX can play a real flute in an expressive way. But the expression does not really come from the robot. It simply does as it is told by a human programmer.

James McLurkin
with his Swarm
Orchestra

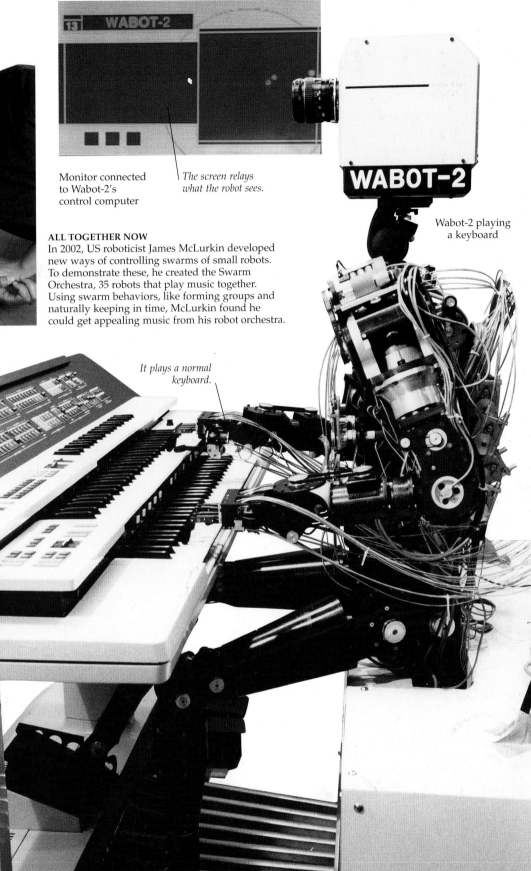

Monitor connected
to Wabot-2's
control computer

*The screen relays
what the robot sees.*

WABOT-2

Wabot-2 playing
a keyboard

ALL TOGETHER NOW
In 2002, US roboticist James McLurkin developed
new ways of controlling swarms of small robots.
To demonstrate these, he created the Swarm
Orchestra, 35 robots that play music together.
Using swarm behaviors, like forming groups and
naturally keeping in time, McLurkin found he
could get appealing music from his robot orchestra.

*It plays a normal
keyboard.*

*The robots have
concealed wheels.*

*Sound wave
generated by a
robot musician.*

FAMOUS FINGERS
One of the better-known
musical robots is Wabot-2.
It was developed at Waseda
University from an earlier
humanoid robot. Playing a
keyboard from sheet music
was an ambitious goal, but by
1984 Wabot-2 was sitting at
an electronic organ, reading
music with its camera eye,
and playing simple tunes. It
could also accompany
singers, by listening
to their voices and
keeping in time.

Animatronics

THE CREATION OF robotic actors is known as animatronics. It is a modern extension of the ancient craft of puppetry. Animatronics uses advanced electronic and mechanical technology to bring astonishing realism to movies, television, and exhibitions. Some animatronic characters are controlled with rods like traditional puppets. Others work by elaborate remote control, which converts the movements of a human directly into the movements of the animatronic character. Animatronic creatures in exhibitions are usually programmed to repeat a sequence of movements.

The sub-skeleton provides support for the skin.

Pneumatic cylinders power the creature's movements.

The frame has numerous moving joints.

1 MOVING PARTS
The animatronic frame is the most important part of the character. Engineers first create virtual models on computers and build small-scale prototypes. When the design is finalized, the metal frame is made in pieces then carefully bolted together.

How it is done

Bringing an extinct animal like this 6.5-ft- (2-m-) tall Megalosaurus back to life is a real challenge for artists, engineers, and computer programmers. The creature is based on a clay model made by sculptors. Mechanical engineers create the skeleton that will allow it to move. Painters are called in to add color to its skin. When all this work is done, animatronics programmers will finally bring movement to the mighty Megalosaur.

The claws are fitted as part of the sub-skeleton.

Fiberglass is used for the sub-skeleton because it is light and strong.

The metal frame and fiberglass moldings combine to create the dinosaur's skeleton.

The mechanics of the frame have to be working perfectly before the sub-skeleton is added.

2 SHAPE AND STRENGTH
Fiberglass moldings, called the sub-skeleton, are added to give the basic frame extra shape and strength. The sub-skeleton is cast in a mold taken from the clay model. The pneumatic cylinders are protected by the framework of the skeleton. These cylinders will later be connected to cables so that they can be controlled electronically.

ALL UNDER CONTROL
Some animatronic characters are brought to life with systems like the Neal Scanlan Studio Performance Animation Controller (PAC). It allows one person to control several actions by converting hand and finger movements into electronic signals that bring the creature to life.

PROBLEMATIC PIGLET
Author Dick King-Smith's book *Babe the Sheep-Pig* – about a talking piglet that could round up sheep – presented a real challenge when it was made into a film in 1995. It took specialists two years to develop an animatronic piglet with a full range of facial expressions.

Babe with Ferdinand—a duck who thinks he's a rooster

The skin is painted by hand with lifelike colors.

The teeth are molded from plastic resin.

Power cables and hoses enter through the dinosaur's feet.

3 SCALES AND WRINKLES
The skin is made of silicone rubber. It is cast from the same detailed mold as the sub-skeleton so that the two fit together perfectly. The textured, rubbery skin is stretched over the skeleton. It has to be flexible enough to allow for realistic movement.

The skin is about 0.5 in (1 cm) thick.

4 READY FOR ACTION
When the entire skeleton has been covered with skin, details like the teeth and tongue are added. The textured skin is then painted. Finally, the pneumatic hoses and electronic control cables that will provide the dinosaur with power are connected.

Machines with feelings

Feelix smiles and raises its eyebrows when it is happy.

SIMPLE SOUL
Jakob Fredslund and Lola Cañamero from Lego-Lab in Denmark created Feelix. It is programmed to react with anger, happiness, or fear when its feet are touched in different ways. Feelix is a simple robot, but it has taught people a great deal about how humans interact with robots that seem to show feelings.

WE OFTEN ATTRIBUTE emotions to machines, saying perhaps that the car is behaving badly when it will not start. Can an inanimate object really have feelings? Modern roboticists are trying to answer this question by building machines that simply act as though they have feelings. This is a response to the fact that, as machines become more complex and powerful, they need richer ways of interacting with human beings. People are more likely to accept robots as part of their life if they can communicate emotionally with them.

The eyebrows are raised.

Kismet looking surprised

Kismet's ears can move to contribute to its expression.

Kismet interacting with Cynthia Breazeal

The eyes are opened wide.

Complex mechanics are needed to produce Kismet's facial expressions.

The mouth is opened wide.

FACE TO FACE
Kismet is a robot capable of face-to-face interaction. It responds to human facial expressions and hand gestures with signals that include gaze direction, facial expression, and vocal babbling. Kismet has mobile ears, eyebrows, eyelids, lips, and jaw. It was designed by Cynthia Breazeal at the Massachusetts Institute of Technology, and has had a huge influence on the world of robotics. Kismet is retired at the Institute's museum.

The mouth is clamped shut.

Kismet expresses sadness by lowering its eyelids and brows and drooping its ears.

Kismet making a sad face

SHY MACHINE

Since Kismet appeared, other researchers have developed similar robots. Waseda University has produced WE-4—a more realistic, but perhaps less appealing, machine. WE-4's face is covered with plastic sheeting that lights up in a blush when the robot is embarrassed. Unlike Kismet, WE-4 has a sense of touch and can also detect the smell of ammonia and cigarettes.

WE-4 can blink as quickly as a human.

The lips are extremely flexible.

A set of mechanical lungs makes WE-4 appear to breathe.

FRIENDLY GUIDE

The robot Sage was used as a tour guide at the Carnegie Museum of Natural History. When its batteries got low, Sage behaved as if it was tired, and a lack of visitors made it lonely. If people got in Sage's way it became angry, but anyone in the way of a lonely Sage made it happy—it was pleased to see them! If museum visitors paid attention to it, it grew cheerful and told jokes. The robot was developed in the 1990s by US engineer Illah Nourbakhsh.

FEELING AT HOME

The Evolution Robotics ER2 was designed to help around the home. It doesn't have a humanoid face, but it has been specifically created to interact with people. Its vision system is good at recognizing faces and gestures, and it comes with basic software that designers can customize to generate different emotions.

Flexible skin and motors modeled on human facial muscles gave My Real Baby hundreds of different expressions.

REALISTIC BABY

My Real Baby was developed in 2000 by toymaker Hasbro and Rodney Brooks, director of the iRobot company. It had an expressive face and voice, and also touch and motion sensors. The doll knew when it was being fed, rocked, or ignored, and it reacted with one of 15 humanlike emotions.

Teams and swarms

THE SMARTEST OF today's robots is only about as intelligent as an ant. This lack of brains could be less of a disadvantage than it seems. Ants, despite their limited intelligence, are highly successful animals. Their secret is to act not as individuals, but as a team. Many other animals, including birds and bees, also benefit from this type of group behavior—forming flocks or swarms increases their chances of survival. Roboticists are beginning to work on this idea, hoping that the group intelligence of a team of small, simple robots can replace the individual intelligence that has proved so elusive for their larger cousins.

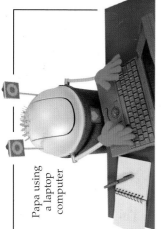

Papa using a laptop computer

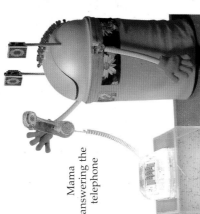

Mama answering the telephone

ACTING TOGETHER
A robot theater created by Ethno-Expo toured Switzerland in 2000–2002. The actors, four Koala robots, could find their places on stage, interact, speak, and move their arms and mouths. Kids and parents loved the play, which was called *Small Children—Joy and Burden.*

Each robot is named after a character from Snow White and the Seven Dwarfs.

The sonar sensors point in three directions.

The foam head is mounted on a wire frame.

BEE TEAM
Bees are great teamworkers; they use smell and waggling dances to communicate with members of their hive. Communication is an essential part of teamwork, even when the team is made up of robots.

Some of the electronics are mounted on a "piggyback" circuit board.

The foam acts as a buffer.

BULLY BOTS
A robot swarm known as the Seven Dwarfs was created in the 1990s. The small, highly mobile robots could communicate with each other using infrared light. Realistic group behavior would often emerge from their very simple programs. On one occasion, a robot blundered into a wall and got stuck. The others crowded around and pushed it back whenever it tried to escape, just like playground bullies! The Seven Dwarfs are still used to teach robotics at Reading University, UK, where they were developed.

The wheels are rubbery to give a good grip on smooth surfaces.

The memory chip holds the robot's program.

The chassis is made from sturdy aluminum.

The robot can be switched off when not in use.

The switches can be set to alter behavior.

SHARED KNOWLEDGE

Tupperbots—robots made with kitchen containers—were built in the 1990s to see if a group of robots could evolve like natural organisms. When they get together, the robots exchange sections of their computer programs. This may create a new program that works better, so that its owner is more likely to survive. Research of this kind is ongoing.

JOINT EFFORT

Swarm-bots are under development in Belgium. They are robot colonies that are made up from smaller, autonomous units called S-bots. The idea is that 30 or so of these will communicate with each other and work together as a Swarm-bot. Unlike a single S-bot, the Swarm-bot will be able to lift heavy objects and bridge chasms.

Pradeep Khosla demonstrates a Millibot

MILITARY MILLIBOTS

Pradeep Khosla at Carnegie Mellon University believes that a team of specialized robots can often do better than a single, larger robot. He is working on a robotic team for military reconnaissance and surveillance. Each little Millibot carries a different sensor, such as a camera or temperature probe. The Millibots can also link together to cross gaps.

Team of Millibots

Cyborgs

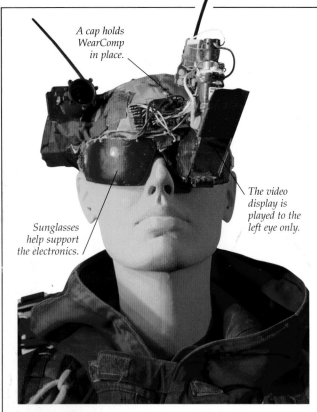

A cap holds *WearComp* in place.

Sunglasses help support the electronics.

The video display is played to the left eye only.

CYBORG MANN
This model is wearing a computer called WearComp. It was developed by Steve Mann, a Canadian engineer and artist, who wears one day and night. WearComp allows him to transmit to the Internet, block unwanted sights, and turn his world into hyperlinks. Mann could be described as the first cyborg—the first person to live in intimate contact with a computer, seeing everything, including himself, through its eyepiece.

IF YOU CAN'T MAKE machines more like people, you can try making people more like machines. The word cyborg (cybernetic organism) was coined by Austrian scientist Manfred Clynes in 1960. His original meaning, of an ability-enhancing partnership between human and machine, has changed to mean something that is part human, part machine. There have been several attempts to make this a reality.

The main problem is that humans and machines work differently. However, both human nerves and computers use electricity to convey their messages, so it is possible to link people and machines electrically.

Engine overlay used by an engineer

Cockpit overlay used by a pilot

VIRTUAL VIEW
Nomad lets engineers view calculations, such as voltage measurements, without putting down their tools to use a computer. Pilots can also use the system to access flight information while keeping their eye on the job.

MICROVISION

The user looks through a transparent screen.

A laser projector produces the images.

Nomad headgear

The headgear contains a battery pack.

QUITE AN EYEFUL
Cyborg technology is now available to the public. The Nomad Augmented Vision System is designed for people who have to use a computer while doing jobs that need both hands. It allows them to work freely without the problems created by a fixed computer. Nomad creates an overlay, or transparent computer screen, that seems to float in front of users wherever they look. It does this by using the eye's own lens to focus the image from a laser right onto the retina.

The electronics communicate with the implanted chip.

The bracelet could be taken on and off, but the chip could only be removed by surgery.

The hand is controlled by signals from Stelarc's muscles.

NERVE LINK
In March 2002, roboticist Kevin Warwick had a microchip implanted in his forearm, with electrodes connecting it to a nerve. He wanted to find out if a computer could make sense of his body's signals, allowing man and machine to work together. Research like this could eventually help people paralyzed by spinal cord damage.

Electronics pick up and translate muscle signals.

CYBORG ARTIST
Stelarc is an Australian artist who uses robotics and the Internet to experiment with extensions to his body. Stelarc has performed with a third hand, a virtual arm, and a virtual body. For one performance he developed a touch-screen muscle stimulator that enabled people to operate his body remotely.

VISION OF THE FUTURE
The Terminator is a fictional character that could, perhaps, be a vision of the distant future. Created in 1984, the cyborg surfaced for the third time in 2003, played, as usual, by Arnold Schwarzenegger. In the movie, he tries to stop evil robot network Skynet from destroying humanity.

Stelarc demonstrates his third hand

An external transmitter sends signals to the implant.

ELECTRONIC EAR
Cyborg technology can help some people who cannot hear. A device called a cochlear implant is embedded in the skull and connected to an external microphone and sound processor. The implant electrically stimulates the nerves in the inner ear, partially restoring the sounds of everyday life, including speech.

Marching machines from *Terminator 3, Rise of the Machines*

Humanoids

A MACHINE THAT looks, thinks, and behaves like a human being has been a dream of artists and engineers for centuries. One reason for this could be that in the process of building such a machine, they would learn a lot about how people work. There are also some practical reasons. A robot shaped like a human being can adapt quite easily to stairs, chairs, and all the other parts of an environment designed for humans. The human body is extremely complex, however, and creating a robot that is capable of simply walking effectively is an enormous challenge.

STREET SMART?
When Tmsuk 04 was let loose on the streets of Japan to see how people reacted, things went seriously wrong. The robot was kicked to "death" by members of the public, suggesting that people are not yet quite ready to live alongside robots.

HONDA WONDER
Asimo is a robot designed to help in the home. It was launched by Honda in 2000 after 14 years of work. Asimo is an unintimidating 4 ft (120 cm) tall. It walks well and turns corners by shifting its center of gravity like a real person. Recent models can recognize human faces and gestures, and can also walk faster than their predecessors.

A battery pack carried on SDR-3X's back provides it with power.

The hands are not jointed and cannot perform tasks.

JUST FOR FUN
After the success of their robot dog, Aibo, Sony launched a humanoid entertainment robot called SDR-3X in 2000. It could get up and walk, balance on one leg, kick a ball, and dance. Its successor, SDR-4X, appeared in 2002. This robot can recognize faces and voices and, with the help of a computer, can talk or even sing.

SDR-3X demonstrating its dancing skills

The joints are extremely mobile.

BARGAIN BOT
Low-cost humanoid Robo Erectus is the work of Singapore engineer Zhou Changjiu. The robot, which was designed to walk and kick balls, came second in the 2002 RoboCup Humanoid Walk League. But Changjiu's real goal is to build a more affordable humanoid.

HELPFUL BUILDER
Morph3 is a 15-in (38-cm) robot intended as a construction kit for the development of humanoid technology. It was made in Japan by Hiroaki Kitano. Morph3 is lightweight and its motors, gears, and sensors can fit together in a variety of different ways.

Pino has a long nose, like its namesake Pinocchio.

Pino stands just 30 in (75 cm) tall.

Morph3 can stand, crouch, and walk smoothly and swiftly.

PERSONAL PLAYER
Hiroaki Kitano developed Pino for RoboCup. Kitano sees its human shape as more than an aid to playing soccer. He thinks that in the future, humans will be more likely to work alongside humanoid robots if they like them. That's why Pino has an appealing shape and a totally unnecessary nose.

Into the future

NO ONE CAN TELL where robotics is leading us. Even experts cannot agree on what the future with robots might be like. Some say we may become dependent on intelligent machines that think for themselves. Others say that robots will never be that sophisticated. This uncertainty centers on a basic question: what is intelligence? If we can find out enough about intelligence to reproduce it with a computer, then we may soon have machines that are smarter than we are. If understanding intelligence proves to be beyond us, however, the sci-fi future of humanoids and cyborgs may elude us forever.

HRP-2's "clothes" can be changed if required.

The wings may be made from ultra-thin metal.

ROBOT WASP
New knowledge is making new kinds of robot possible. Scientists have recently figured out exactly how insect wings work, while engineers are developing nanotechnology—ways of making very small objects. Together, these could produce insect-sized robots in the future—some as fearsome as this computer-generated wasp.

MIGHTY MECHA
This could be the worker of the future. Seen here in its 2003 Mecha costume, HRP-2 is being developed by Kawada Industries in Japan. Their aim is to build a robot that can operate on a real building site. HRP-2 stands 5 ft 1 in (154 cm) tall, and is one of only two humanoid robots that can get up unaided if it falls over.

Harmful organisms in the path of the nanobot

IN THE BLOOD
Nanotechnology could bring great medical advances in the future. Nanorobots small enough to pass through blood vessels, and armed with chemical weapons, could seek out and destroy deadly bacteria and viruses. The robots could even be trained to group together after the job was done and exit at a chosen point so that they could be used again.

Jointed ankles give it a smooth walking action.

Sonar transmitters and receivers are located on the front of the head.

Video cameras are mounted in the eye sockets.

HOUSEHOLD HELP
Home robots of the future may look humanoid, like this computer image, but are just as likely to look like refrigerators on wheels. They are unlikely to wield a normal mop and bucket, but they should be able to do more than today's robot vacuums and lawnmowers.

MAGIC MORGUI
K-28, or Morgui (Chinese for "magic ghost"), a new robot at Reading University, UK, is a scary skull whose gaze really does follow you around the room. It can even make a video recording of you while it does this. But K-28 has a serious purpose. Equipped with sight, hearing, infrared, radar, and sonar, it is being used in research that will enable future robots to combine all these senses much more effectively.

Microphones are positioned where human ears would be.

FUTURE FEAR
Some experts have suggested that robots could become as intelligent as humans in the not-too-distant future. Unless we take urgent action, they claim, the robots might take over. But this is just one view. Other experts dismiss it as fantasy, saying that while computers are advancing rapidly, our knowledge of how to use them lags far behind.

march of the
machines
WHY THE NEW RACE OF ROBOTS
WILL RULE THE WORLD
Kevin Warwick

The parts are linked by magnets.

Infrared sensors are positioned on the top lip.

The smaller parts are referred to as "female."

"We're going to see machines that are more intelligent than we are perhaps by 2030… how are we going to cope with that?"

KEVIN WARWICK
Professor of Cybernetics, Reading University, UK

SHAPE SHIFTERS
What shape will tomorrow's robots be? They will be whatever shape they need to be, if Daniela Rus of Dartmouth College gets her way. She is one of several roboticists working on robots that can change their shape for different jobs. Their bodies are made of separate parts that can slide and link in various ways to change shape in seconds.

Index

Acknowledgments

The Publishers would like to thank the following for their kind permission to reproduce their photographs:
Abbreviations: a: above, b: below, c: center, l: left, r: right, t: top
Photo courtesy of ActivMedia Robotics, www.MobileRobots.com: 2cr, 4br, 24cr, trc, 25tl; Thanks to Advanced Design, Inc. (www.robix.com) for the use of their Robix ™ RCS-6 robot construction set: 27; Courtesy of Aerosonde: 42c, cb; AKG Images: 11tl, 36tl; Courtesy of AUVSI.org: 45bl; BBC Picture Archives: 30–31b; Robot Sculptures made by Clayton G. Bailey, Port Costa, CA, courtesy of http://claytonbailey.com: 48br; John Kittelsrud—Botbash Robotic Combat Sports: 30cr; Burden Neurological Institute: 12c; Paul Spooner/Cabaret Mechanical Theatre 2000, photo: Heini Schneebeli: 11br; Carnegie Mellon, Photo: Ken Andreyo: 57bl, bc; Central Art Archives, Kenneth Rinaldo "Autopoiesis" in the exhibition "Alien Intelligence" in the Museum of Contemporary Art Kiasma, Helsinki 2000. Photo: Petri Virtanen: 48tl; Courtesy of Century, photographer Simon Battensby: 63cr; Corbis: 44–45, 45br, 50c, tl, 51cl, 63tr; Forrest J. Ackerman Collection: 8c; Archivo Iconografico SA: 30tl; Joe Bator: 43tl; Annebicque Bernard/Sygma: 41l; Bettmann: 6tr, 13l, 26tl, 28l, 32tl; Duomo: 32tc; Pitchal Frederic/Sygma: 33tl; Francetelecom/IRCAD/ Sygma: 18br; Laurence Kesterson/Sygma: 18cl; James Leynse/Saba: 20t, 21cra; Joe McDonald: 56tl; Roger Ressmeyer: 34tl, 38br; Sygma: 53tr; Soqui Ted/Sygma: 30cl; Bill Varie: 34–35;

Haruyoshi Yamaguchi/Sygma: 1, 32tr, 33tr, 60tr, b; Courtesy of the Defense Advanced Research Projects Agency: 43tc, tr, br, 42–43; Eaglemoss International Ltd./www.realrobots. co.uk/Simon Anning: 15tl; Electrolux: 18br, 39tr; ER2, a prototype service robot developed by Evolution Robotics, and Idealab company based in Pasadena, CA: 2tc, 55cr; Photo: Elvira Anstmann, © Ethno-Expo Zurich: 56tr, cr; Mary Evans Picture Library: 6tl, 10tl, tr, 20l, 38tl, 39tl; © Jakob Fredslund: 54tl; Courtesy of FriendlyRobotics: 39br; Courtesy of Fujitsu Ltd.: 39bc; Hulton Archive/Getty Images: 24tr; MY REAL BABY is a trademark of Hasbro and is used with permission. © 2003 Hasbro. All rights reserved: 55br; Dr. J. B. C. Davies, Heriot-Watt University: 45cr; Honda (UK): 4 bl, 60tl; © Team Shredder, UK: 31 tl, tr, cl; Courtesy of Peter Rowe, Dave Pearson of Kawasaki Robotics Ltd.: 20r; Thanks to Kate Howey Elgan Loane of Kentree Ltd., Ireland: 22cr, c, bl; Kitano Symbiotic Systems Project: 61br, Designer Shunjo Yamanaka, Photo Yukio Shimizu: 61 tl; Courtesy of Keith Kotay, Dartmouth Robotics Laboratory, NH: 63br; K-Team S.A., Switzerland: 2bl, 25; © 2003 The Lego Group: 2cl, 4crb, 27bl; LEGO, the LEGO logo and the brick configuration are trademarks of the LEGO Group and are used here with permission: 32–33; Courtesy of Steve Mann: 58tl; Courtesy of Microvision, Inc.: 58bl, br, cr, tr; Photo: Paul Miller: 26cl; Dug North Automata: 48c; Courtesy of Lucent Technologies: 13c; Courtesy of the Laser

and Electronics Group, Mitsubishi Heavy Industries Ltd. Japan: 4cra, 38bl; Courtesy of Hans Moravec: 43cr, bl; Museum of the Moving Image: 9bl; NASA: 42tr, 46b, clb, t, 47b, tr; NASA Ames Research Center: 27r; National Museum of Japanese History: 11tr; Natural Environment Research Council, and Nick Millard of Southampton Oceanography Center: 45t; Nature Picture Library: © Mark Brownlow: 44tr; Photo: Mark Ostow: 51tl; PA Photos: EPA-UK: 29cl, 50cl; A. K. Peters, Ltd., publisher of Mobile Robots: Inspiration to Implementation by Joseph Jones, Anita Flynn and Bruce Seiger: 27tl; The Picture Desk: Advertising Archives Ltd.: 22tl; The Art Archive/Victoria and Albert Museum London/Sally Chappell: 10–11; Kobal Collection: Lucas Film/20th Century Fox: 8r; ORION: 9tl; TRI-STAR: 9br; Rex Features: 7r; Action Press: 22–23c; Nigel Dickinson: 20–21c; David James: 18cr; Nils Jorgensen: 29tr; Masatoshi Okauchi: 50bl, 51br, 62l; Warner Br/Everett: 59bl; Christian Ristow: 48bl; Courtesy of robotlab/www.robotlab.de: 49bl, br; PAC, courtesy of Neal Scanlan Studio: 53tl; Science Photo Library: Delphine Aures/Eurelios: 57c; Claude Charlier: 36cl; Colin Cuthbert: 44bl; European Space Agency: 47cr; Mauro Fermariello: 35tr; Astrid and Hans Frieder Michler: 62–63; A Gragera/ Latin Stock: 44bc; Adam Hart-Davis: 17t; James King-Holmes: 59bl; Mehau Kulyk: 18tl; Lawrence Livermore National Laboratory: 42tl; Los Alamos National Laboratory: 12tc; Peter Menzel: 17cl, 19bl, 29ca, 36–37b, 41t, 44tl, 51r, 55tr; Rob Michelson/GTRI: 47tl; Miximilian Stock Ltd.: 7tl; Hank Morgan: 41bl, 49tl, tr; NASA: 23tl, 46cl; NASA/

Carnegie Mellon University: 23br; Sam Ogden: 19cr, 23 cl, tr, 54cr, bl, br; Philippe Plailly/Eurelios: 25tr; H. Raguet/Eurelios: 37tr; Volker Steger: 36bl, c, 41br; Taquet, Jerrican: 7c; Mark Thomas: 19tl; Victor Habbick Visions: 62br, cr; Peter Yates: 17bl; Ed Young/AGStock: 21cra; Science & Society Picture Library: 12tr; Science Museum: 44br, cr; SelecT ™—the first automated solution to culture 1 to 182 cell lines simultaneously and generate assay-ready plates. www.automation partnership.com: 35cr; © Shadow Robot Company: 15tr; School of Electrical and Electronic Engineering, Singapore Polytechnic: 61tr; Dave Hrynkiw, Solarbotics Ltd.: 14tr; SRI International: 4 cl, 13cr, 24cl; Swarm-bots are designed and produced within the "SWARM-BOTS" project (www.swarm-bots.org), a European Commission project funded within the Future Emerging Technologies program: 57br; tmsuk Co. Japan: 5tr, 38–39; Quadruped wall-climbing robot "NINJA-II" developed in Hirose laboratory of Tokyo Institute of Technology, http://mozu.mes. titech.ac.jp/hirohome.html: 40b; Courtesy of the Department of Electrical and Electronic Engineering, University of Portsmouth: 40t; University of Reading: Courtesy of the Department of Cybernetics: 63l; courtesy of Kevin Warwick: 59t; University of Westminster: 13br; US Department of Defense: 42cr; Courtesy of Valiant Technology, www.valiant-technology. com: 26bl, c, bc; Waseda University: Humanoid Robotics Institute: 51r; Atsuo Takanishi Lab: 55l; © 2003 V & W Animatronics: 52l, r, 53cl, br